Free Yourself from

DEATH ANXIETY

Free
Yourself
from

DEATH ANXIETY

A **CBT** Self-Help Guide for a Fear of Death and Dying

Rachel E. Menzies and David Veale

Jessica Kingsley Publishers
London and Philadelphia

First published in Great Britain in 2022 by Jessica Kingsley Publishers
An imprint of Hodder & Stoughton Ltd
An Hachette Company

2

Disclaimer: The information contained in this book is not intended to replace the services of trained medical professionals or to be a substitute for medical advice. You are advised to consult a doctor on any matters relating to your health, and in particular on any matters that may require diagnosis or medical attention.

A CIP catalogue record for this title is available from the British Library and the Library of Congress

ISBN 978 1 78775 814 8
eISBN 978 1 78775 815 5

Printed and bound in Great Britain by Bell & Bain Limited

Jessica Kingsley Publishers' policy is to use papers that are natural, renewable and recyclable products and made from wood grown in sustainable forests. The logging and manufacturing processes are expected to conform to the environmental regulations of the country of origin.

Jessica Kingsley Publishers
Carmelite House
50 Victoria Embankment
London EC4Y 0DZ

www.jkp.com

Contents

Acknowledgements

We would like to acknowledge our clinical colleagues (especially Professors Mark Freeston, Paul Salkovskis, Paul Gilbert and Ross Menzies) and people with death anxiety whom we have treated, who have given their valuable time and feedback to help us with this book. You are the inspiration in making this work accessible so that more people with death anxiety can achieve meaningful goals and live a life without fear.

Please note that the worksheets marked with ✳ are available to download and print from https://library.jkp.com/redeem using the voucher code USGVCPX.

———

CHAPTER 1

What is Death Anxiety?

Introduction

Death anxiety is a term used to describe people's fear or negative feelings towards death or dying. It is part of being human but becomes a problem when it is sufficiently time consuming, distressing or interfering in one's life.

Death anxiety is expressed in many different ways. Some people may focus on their own death, ruminating on all the things they will miss out on after they die, or what it will be like to not exist any more. Some people may experience doubts about the nature of existence itself, questioning what will happen to them after death or obsessing over whether they will exist in a parallel world. Others may worry about the process of dying and whether their death will be painful, or what their final moments will be like. Other people may not worry about their own death at all. Instead, they might find themselves distressed at the idea of losing a loved one. They may worry about how they will cope with their loved one's death or may even worry that they will somehow cause the death of their loved one without meaning to. For some there is a phobic avoidance and fear of anything related to death. All of the experiences above are in many ways part of being human, but death anxiety is a problem when it becomes extremely time consuming, distressing or interfering in your life.

You may have heard about other older names for the fear of death, such as 'necrophobia' (derived from the Greek *nekros* meaning 'corpse'), and 'thanatophobia' (from the Greek *Thanatos*, the god of death in ancient Greek mythology). 'Death anxiety' is the term most often used and most easily understood, and so we will stick to this term for the sake of simplicity.

Who experiences death anxiety?

An awareness and fear of death is part of being human. As you will see in the next chapter, death anxiety is wired into us. Being scared of death has kept our species alive for thousands of years, making it a very common and normal thing to experience. What's more, it can be very difficult to truly imagine or accept that we are mortal. More than a century ago, Freud acknowledged that 'It is indeed impossible to imagine our own death', because 'whenever we attempt to do so we can perceive that we are in fact still present as spectators'.[1] The idea that we will one day die can seem so strange and incomprehensible, that 'At bottom, no one believes in his own death... Every one of us is convinced of his own immortality.'[2]

We all have an innate tendency to fear death and refuse to accept it. However, although this fear is a pervasive one, we might still experience death anxiety differently from the people around us. For example, we know that death anxiety is generally more common in women than men. We also know that religion plays a role in who experiences death anxiety (although, as you will see

---

1   Freud, S. (1957). 'Thoughts for the times on war and death.' In *The Standard Edition of the Complete Psychological Works of Sigmund Freud,* Vol. 14. London: Hogarth Press, p.289.
2   Page 41 of the same volume.

in the next chapter, having strong religious beliefs does not necessarily protect people from fears of death).

You can think of death anxiety as existing on a spectrum. Some people will feel quite comfortable with death, whereas most people will feel at least a little anxious about it. For others, their fear of death may be very distressing, and might be interfering with their ability to enjoy life, to build healthy relationships or to achieve meaningful goals.

Other emotions

Although the term 'death anxiety' seems to only refer to feeling anxious or fearful about death, people may also experience other emotions. For instance, some people describe feeling angry or sad about death. For our purposes, we will also include these other emotions under the umbrella term of 'death anxiety' throughout this book.

How to use this book

This book has primarily been written for people who feel fearful of death or dying. You may choose to work through the book independently, using it as a self-help guide. Alternatively, you might choose to use it alongside therapy you're currently undergoing, and to discuss the content and the exercises in the book with your therapist. That being said, you do not need to have a therapist, or a mental health disorder, to benefit from reading this book.

We have included lots of practical tips on how to overcome your death anxiety in this book. You might be tempted to skip straight to the later chapters to find out how you can start to make changes. However, we recommend that you start the book at the beginning and read it through in order. This is because we find that a good understanding of your problems and how they are maintained helps you to know exactly what needs to change.

We have also included spaces for you to reflect on your own personal experiences, and to help develop your understanding of key ideas throughout the book. We find that the more time you take to complete the exercises, the more you will get out of the chapters and the information provided.

Lastly, we have used characters throughout the book to help explain ideas and to apply them to real life. These characters are fictional but based on the common problems that arise in people with death anxiety. Although we have tried to choose examples that represent some of the features of death anxiety, every person's experience of the condition will be unique to them. You might struggle with entirely different aspects of death anxiety from those reflected in our characters. This does not mean that you are alone in your own experience of death anxiety. There will likely be some similarities in the processes that maintain your fears, and it will still be helpful to follow the same principles outlined in the book.

How do I know if I have death anxiety?

Let's take a look at some of the common ways that death anxiety can appear.

Tick any of the following that you do:

☐ Spend lots of time each day thinking about death, either my own or someone else's (e.g. to the point where it is making it difficult to enjoy the present moment, focus on work, or attend to relationships or responsibilities).

☐ Experience distressing images which pop into my head about possible ways of dying or what might happen after death.

☐ Avoid things that I think could cause death, which other people do not typically avoid (e.g. flying, driving, eating certain foods, leaving the house).

☐ Avoid anything that reminds me of death (e.g. walking past cemeteries, visiting hospitals or medical centres, watching films or TV shows about death), pushing away thoughts of death when they arise.

☐ Excessively seek reassurance that my loved ones and I are safe and healthy (e.g. asking loved ones or medical specialists, or googling symptoms or other health-related things online).

☐ Compulsively do things which I believe will keep me healthy and safe (e.g. excessively exercise, over-prepare for 'worst-case scenarios', repeat certain phrases or perform certain 'rituals').

☐ Try to get more information to obtain certainty about death or the outcome after death (e.g. repeatedly search on the internet for experiences of or views on what happens after death).

☐ Act in ways to try and improve the outcome after death, such as behaving in a way which will be judged as 'good' or moral.

If you have ticked any of the above boxes, this may be a sign of death anxiety.

When does death anxiety become a problem?

It's a problem if it is significantly distressing, time consuming or starting to get in the way of your life and interfere with your relationships, friendships, family life, work or education.

> Are your fears about death significantly distressing? Does your death anxiety get in the way of your life? How would your life be different if you were able to overcome this fear?
>
> ....
>
> ....
>
> ....
>
> ....

Throughout this book, we introduce various strategies and approaches to help you overcome your fear of death. To help illustrate some of these important points, we use the experiences of five different people to offer real-world examples of the different forms that death anxiety can take. These five characters are fictional but have been drawn from our experiences working with a number of people with death anxiety.

Marianne

Marianne is a 38-year-old woman, who is the primary carer for her two young children. Marianne's fear of death began after the birth of her first child, when she began to worry what might happen to her daughter if she suddenly died. Although her husband tries to reassure her that her children would be in good hands, Marianne can't shake the feeling that her children's lives would be ruined if she were to suddenly die. Because of this fear, she tries to stay at home whenever she can, to 'stay out of harm's way'. In addition to worrying about her own death, she also worries that something might happen to her children. As a result, Marianne rarely lets them out of her sight and is always on the lookout for any sign of illness. The minute that one of her children complains of a headache or stomach ache, she is filled with panic, and rushes them to her local medical centre, or spends hours googling their symptoms. Although Marianne would like to return to work, she worries about leaving her children in day care, and is anxious that they might get a stomach bug or be injured. She has also become very isolated, as her anxiety makes it difficult to go out in public and meet friends the way she used to.

Peter

Peter is a 34-year-old man, who works in publishing. Peter's worries about death began after a psychedelic drug experience in which he felt that he was actually dying. Since then, the idea of death has caused him severe anxiety. In particular, he is terrified by the idea of non-existence, and struggles to accept that he will not think or feel anything after death. When he feels anxious about this, he feels compelled to check online forums to see whether other people have a solution to this problem. On his better days, he finds himself compulsively checking whether he is truly calm, 'testing out' how he feels about non-existence, which then stirs up more anxiety. As a result of Peter's fixation on his eventual non-existence, he has started to feel that life is pointless. He can't shake the feeling that if life is going to end one day, then his work and day-to-day activities are meaningless. Because of this, his mood has started to worsen, and he has begun to distance himself from other people and withdraw from things he used to enjoy, like sport and watching movies.

Ali

Ali is a 44-year-old man, who works in marketing. Ali can't pinpoint exactly when his death anxiety became a problem. He recalls that he started to become fixated on his health during secondary school, and that it slowly got worse over the years. His worries have varied since then. At one point, he became obsessed with air pollution, and checked the pollution levels in his city each day. He worried that going outside or driving through polluted areas, even for a few minutes, could make him sick. At other times, he has worried about asbestos, or catching HIV. During these periods, he would excessively wash his hands and avoid using public toilets or walking near building sites or old buildings. A few years ago, he started to experience heart flutters, which sent him into a panic. He visited a number of cardiologists, and each told him that it was just a cardiac arrhythmia and was harmless. Even so, Ali feels very anxious whenever he notices it, and avoids activities like exercise which he thinks will exacerbate it. He often spends a few times each day checking whether his heart is beating 'normally'. Ali's anxiety has also stopped him travelling the way he used to. Although he used to be adventurous, Ali now refuses to travel anywhere where he feels medical help would not be available if he had a sudden heart attack. As a result, he often plans out his routes before going anywhere, to ensure there is a hospital nearby.

Sasha

Sasha is a 21-year-old woman, who is studying architecture. Sasha has always been an anxious person. When she was a child, she used to worry about robbers breaking in, and monsters hiding under her bed. In her late teens, she saw her grandmother die in hospital and this brought on a lot of worries about death. In particular, Sasha worries about her parents dying, and how she will cope when that happens. She is very close to her parents and is terrified that she will completely fall apart when they die. As a result, she frequently tries to check on their safety, for example calling them when they are running late on their way home from work. Often when she is watching a movie or TV show and death is mentioned, she gets an intrusive image of her parents on their deathbed. When this happens, she instantly tries to push the thought away, and often turns off the movie. She also sometimes worries about all the ways that they could die, such as from a natural disaster, illness or being attacked. Sometimes she feels that worrying about these things helps her prepare for their death, even though she usually just ends up feeling terribly sad and anxious.

Julie

Julie is a 56-year-old woman. She has two adult children, and lives with her husband, Micah. A few years ago, she was diagnosed with stage III ovarian cancer. She underwent a year of intensive treatment, including chemotherapy and surgery. Although this was a difficult period, particularly given the side effects of the treatment, Julie remained optimistic. For a while, her cancer went into remission, and it looked as if she would completely recover. Then, ten months ago, a scan revealed that the cancer had advanced and had now spread to her liver. Julie was told that she would have only a few years to live. Ever since this news, Julie has felt completely overwhelmed with the idea of dying. She feels terrified at the thought that her life will be cut short so soon. Julie also finds herself stewing on her 'mistakes' and things she has done in the past and worries that she might go to hell. Although her husband Micah is supportive and tries to remind her that these things are not as bad as she feels, she finds it hard to believe him. Micah is becoming frustrated that Julie refuses to sit down and discuss her will and funeral wishes with him. Although she knows this will be helpful, she can't bear to face it, and feels that she will not cope with the anxiety it brings up in her. She has found herself becoming more and more isolated, and has started to avoid seeing her children, in case they want to talk to her about the future. Julie feels hopeless knowing her life is destined to end in the next few years.

Understanding your death anxiety

In order to treat any problem, we first have to understand it. When it comes to fears of death, it is important to identify your thoughts, emotions and behaviours first in order to address your death anxiety. As you will see throughout this book, our thoughts and beliefs are linked to how we *feel* about death, and also how we *behave*. We will be using the examples of Marianne, Peter, Ali, Sasha, and Julie to help explain the common emotions, thoughts and behaviours that come up for people with death anxiety.

Thoughts about death

Identifying your thoughts about death is a crucial step in working towards freeing yourself from fears of death. These may be intrusive thoughts which automatically pop into your head (e.g. 'Wouldn't it be awful if I had a heart attack and died right now?') or they might be beliefs which you have held strongly for a long time (e.g. 'Life is meaningless if it all one day comes to an end'). In addition to the examples given here, a survey assessing some unhelpful beliefs about death can be found in the Appendix.

Thoughts about death often fall into the categories listed here.

Thoughts about one's own death

The following are all examples of thoughts about one's own death (i.e. one's own non-existence, rather than the process of dying, which we will discuss next):

- Thoughts about how bad it would be to not experience anything ever again (e.g. 'It would be awful to miss out on seeing my children grow up' or, 'It will be horrible to stop existing, or to never think, feel or speak again').
- Thoughts about not being ready to die, or needing to 'tick off' certain goals or leave a legacy behind (e.g. 'I must accomplish all my goals before I die' or, 'It would be horrible to die before I've done things I want to').
- Thoughts about your own death negatively impacting loved ones (e.g. 'My death would destroy my daughter's life' or, 'My partner would never recover if I died suddenly' or, 'I need to stop myself from dying so I can take care of my family' or, 'It will be horrible to see loved ones being upset and not knowing how to comfort them').
- Thoughts about how others will view us after death (e.g. 'I need to be remembered after I die' or, 'Nobody will miss me when I die').

Thoughts about the process of dying

As opposed to the above list of thoughts about one's own death, thoughts about the process of dying centre on the experience of dying; that is, what the final moments of life might look like, the method of dying, and how it would feel to die. These include:

- Thoughts about dying being painful or unpleasant (e.g. 'Dying will involve terrible pain and suffering' or, 'I won't be able to cope on my deathbed' or, 'It would be humiliating to depend on others as I'm dying').

- Thoughts about specific methods from which one might die (e.g. 'I couldn't cope if I was diagnosed with a terminal illness' or, 'I am going to die in a plane crash' or, 'It would be horrible to die alone').

Thoughts about losing a loved one

Thoughts about losing a loved one are common in death anxiety. These may include thoughts about the loss itself, one's ability to cope with that loss or the dying process of a loved one. For example:

- Thoughts about struggling to cope with a death (e.g. 'If my partner were to die suddenly, it would destroy me' or, 'I could not accept the finality of the death of my parent' or, 'I would never recover after the death of my child').
- Thoughts about witnessing the dying process of a loved one (e.g. 'I couldn't cope with being by the bedside of a dying family member' or, 'It would be horrible to know that a loved one was going to die soon').

Thoughts about needing to control or prevent death

- Thoughts about needing to influence death beyond what is possible, often in a magical way (e.g. 'I have to think positively to prevent death').
- Thoughts about needing control of the dying process (e.g. 'I need to have complete control over how I die').

Thoughts about needing certainty over what will happen

- Thoughts about needing certainty on the aftermath of death (e.g. 'I need to know whether there is life after death').
- Thoughts about how one will die ('I need to know for sure how I'm going to die').

Thoughts about death as a whole

These thoughts are often quite broad, sweeping statements about death in general. They include:

- Thoughts about death being generally unfair, unnatural, untimely or otherwise bad (e.g. 'I shouldn't have to die' or, 'Death is always a tragedy' or, 'Life is far too short').

Thoughts about dead bodies and places related to death

- Thoughts about the awfulness of dead bodies, cemeteries, funeral parlours or anything associated with death.

You now are familiar with some common thoughts that play a role in death anxiety. Once we can understand our thoughts about death, it will help us figure out what it is about death that truly troubles us. In a moment, we will ask you to try and identify your own most distressing thoughts.

Marianne defines her most distressing thought as being:

- *'What if I died suddenly? My children's lives will be destroyed.'*
- *'My children are going to fall ill and die.'*

Peter defines his most distressing thought as being:

- *'It will be horrible to never experience anything again when I die.'*

Ali defines his most distressing thought as being:

- *'I'm going to die suddenly, and it will be horribly painful.'*
- *'I shouldn't have to die. I need to prevent death at all costs.'*

Sasha defines her most distressing thought as being:

- *'I will completely fall apart when my parents die.'*

Julie defines her most distressing thought as being:

- *'I will go to hell when I die.'*
- *'There's no point to anything I do if I'm going to die in a few years.'*

Try to define your most distressing thoughts and worries about death below.

....

....

....

....

....

....

Ruminations

Rumination is a type of thinking which is repetitive, negative and may be self-critical or abstract. Rumination can also be referred to as brooding, analysing, over-thinking or intellectualizing. It means living in your head rather than living in the outside world. For example, someone might stew on past events, 'If only I had never got cancer' or, 'Why am I not making the most of what I have?' Of course, these questions are abstract and do not have an answer.

Can you identify any ruminations in the form of 'Why' or 'If only' type questions about the past or how you feel?

....

....

....

....

Another common repetitive thinking process is worry. Worry is about the future and usually takes the form of 'What if?' statements (e.g. 'What if I rot in hell?' 'What if my child dies in her sleep tonight?' or, 'What will my last moments look like?'). Sometimes, we might even worry about our worrying (e.g. 'What if I have a heart attack and die from all this worrying?'). On a similar note, obsessional doubts (i.e. repeated and excessive questioning or doubting) are driven by a need for certainty (e.g. 'Could I have caused harm?' or, 'Are you absolutely sure that I do not have cancer?').

Can you identify any worry ruminations in the form of 'What if'
or 'Could' doubts about the future?

....

....

....

....

....

....

....

A helpful step is to identify the motivation behind your ruminating
or worrying – for example, you might believe that over-thinking
will help to solve the problem. This will be important in future
chapters in understanding whether your strategy is really in keeping with your values and what's important in life.

For example, Marianne defines her motivation to worry about
the future of her children as a way of trying to problem solve and
keep them safe.

Peter defines his motivation to ruminate about life after death
as a way of trying to prepare himself for the future.

Ali defines his approach as a way of trying to prevent death.

Sasha defines her thinking about her parents' death as trying
to keep herself safe in the future.

Julie defines her thinking about going to hell as a way of trying
to punish herself.

If you are ruminating or excessively worrying, can you identify the motivation behind it? One way of doing this is to ask yourself: What do you fear would happen if you stopped ruminating or worrying?

....

....

....

....

Images around death

An intrusive image refers to a picture or impression that just pops into your mind, especially when you are more anxious about dying. Pictures are powerful. They can encapsulate in a snapshot a multitude of ideas and emotions in a much more vivid way than mental thoughts alone. This also means they can pack a much more powerful emotional punch. For example, you might have a mental picture of dying or being in hell. People often experience such images from an observer perspective; that is, looking back at oneself. For example, one woman had an image of herself dead with her soul floating in space. This was scary for her as she felt she would still be having thoughts and feelings but not be in control of the situation around her. Another example is a man who had images of himself dying painfully and alone. For him, this was a prediction of the future. Images are not always 'pictures' in your mind. They can, for example, be a felt impression of a touch or smell or bodily sensation.

Images usually feel as if they are true or accurate and relevant now. Such pictures are sometimes emotionally linked to bad experiences and are like ghosts from the past, which have not been updated. Thus, if you have had a bad experience of a traumatic accident or illness in the family, then that memory can become stuck in time and now influences the present. Treating images as relevant to your present can create many problems, as well as them not being updated from the past. Such images can shape our behaviour as well as our feelings. If they feel truer than thoughts alone, you might also act as if they are true and try to prevent them from happening. Furthermore, a powerful negative image might intrude when you are trying to think of alternative, more helpful or realistic beliefs about death.

Change involves recognizing that you are just experiencing a picture in your mind and not current reality. Remember that the image is simply a creation of your brain and is not an actual premonition about the future. Instead of trying to suppress the image, it can be helpful simply to refocus your attention on the present moment and your surroundings. It might also involve facing the feared image, as you will see in later chapters.

Do you experience any intrusive images about death? Try to identify them here and what they mean to you. Do they feel as if they have a sense of 'nowness'?

....

....

....

....

Emotions about death

Our thoughts about any given thing are linked to how we feel about it (you will learn more about this in later chapters). The same applies to death; our *thoughts* about death are associated with which *emotion* we feel towards it. For now, let's identify some of the different emotions that commonly come up for people who experience death anxiety.

For many people who feel uncomfortable with death, their dominant emotion is *anxiety*. This is associated with feeling fearful or worried about death. Anxiety can be experienced as sudden and intense (like that felt in a panic attack), accompanied by physical sensations such as a racing heart, trembling, sweating and shortness of breath. As you will learn in the next chapter, anxiety is related to our 'fight or flight' system and is there to prepare you for a perceived threat. You might also experience lower level anxiety, which can feel like physical tension and being unable to relax.

Another common emotion is *sadness*. Sadness can also be experienced intensely (e.g. when we are crying heavily), or at lower levels (e.g. when we are feeling a little down, or blue). People might feel sad at the thought of living without someone they love or imagining how others will feel after they die (e.g. if we think nobody will miss us). Sadness might also be experienced when we see something as meaningless. Note that sadness is different from depression which is emotional numbness and not being able to enjoy pleasure or satisfaction.

Another emotion that people often feel when it comes to death is *anger*. Anger often feels physically similar to anxiety, and may be experienced as a racing heart, muscle tension and clenched jaw or fist. This can range from mild irritation to full-blown rage. We feel angry when we perceive that our goals or values have been blocked or violated, or when we sense some kind of injustice. For example, people might feel angry when they feel that death is unfair, or that it shouldn't happen. If you notice a lot of 'shoulds' in your thoughts (e.g. 'I shouldn't have to die', 'People shouldn't talk about death', 'I should have full control over death'), this is usually a sign that you're experiencing anger.

Alongside these emotions, some people may also experience *guilt*. We experience guilt when we believe that we are responsible for some kind of bad outcome. So, we might feel guilt about death if we feel we would be a burden on others if we died, or if our death were to somehow impact other people in a negative way (such as by leaving loved ones behind). The function of guilt is to communicate to ourselves that we have acted in a way which we don't approve of, and to motivate us to try and make amends or prevent the bad outcome from happening.

Sometimes people might also feel *disgust*, which is characterized by a feeling of revulsion, mild nausea and a desire to distance ourselves from the thing we are disgusted by. For example, we might feel disgusted by the image or presence of things associated with death, such as the sight of a dead animal or blood, or the image of someone who is very ill. The function of disgust is to stop us getting close to things we view as harmful or contagious.

Marianne defines her most dominant emotions as anxiety and guilt.

Peter defines his most dominant emotion as anxiety.

Ali defines his most dominant emotion as anxiety and anger.

Sasha defines her most dominant emotions as sadness and anxiety.

Julie defines her most dominant emotions as anxiety, guilt and depression.

It can be helpful to identify and distinguish your own emotions. If you find it difficult to label your own emotions, we recommend you watch the animated film *Inside Out* (2015),[3] which does an excellent job at explaining how we experience common emotions.

---

3 Docter, P. (Director). (2015). *Inside Out* [Film]. Walt Disney Pictures/Pixar Animation Studios.

Write down the most dominant emotions that you experience when you think about death. For example, when you notice the thoughts you wrote down above, what emotion do these thoughts bring up?

....

....

....

....

Avoidance behaviours

Avoidance is a central part of death anxiety. Nearly everyone who is fearful of death will avoid situations, places or thoughts to stop themselves feeling anxious. Here are some examples of things people with death anxiety commonly avoid:

- Places associated with death (e.g. cemeteries, churches, funerals, funeral parlours, hospitals and nursing homes)
- Things with the perceived potential to cause death (e.g. flying, heights, driving, contaminating substances such as germs, being outside the house, being alone)
- Films or television shows that feature death
- Talking with people about death
- Watching the news
- Preparing a will or discussing end-of-life preferences
- Reading articles about death (e.g. news about celebrity deaths, natural disasters, pandemics, or articles about the dying process)

- Images or symbols of death (e.g. skulls, coffins, tombstones)
- Thoughts of death.

Although this list provides examples of the most common forms of avoidance, it is not exhaustive. Some people may binge eat or use alcohol or drugs to suppress their thoughts related to death. There are an infinite number of things we might avoid out of our fear of death. Regardless of the specific thing avoided, it is important to understand that while avoidance temporarily reduces anxiety, it worsens it in the long term. Avoidance strengthens fears of death, as well as restricting normal life. You may like to refer to the questionnaire in the Appendix, to note how often you avoid death-related situations.

Safety-seeking behaviours

Safety-seeking behaviours (also known as 'safety behaviours' for short) are things that you do when you cannot avoid what you fear. For example, imagine that you worry about flying, because you fear that the plane will crash. When you do need to fly, you might do things like carry some kind of 'lucky' item with you for protection. Or, you might turn away from a funeral parlour that you are passing. These are examples of safety-seeking behaviours.

People use safety-seeking behaviours because they think they will keep them safe and prevent the thing they fear from happening. In fact, the opposite is true. Like avoidance behaviours, safety behaviours will worsen your anxiety in the long term.

If you are unsure about whether something is a safety behaviour, ask yourself: Why do I do this action? What do I fear will happen if I don't do it? If you do the behaviour to prevent a feared outcome (e.g. death or dying or having to think about it), then it is probably a safety behaviour.

Marianne identifies her most frequently used avoidance and safety-seeking behaviours as:

1. *Avoiding leaving my children with other carers.*
2. *Avoiding leaving the house unless I need to.*
3. *In public, always carrying hand sanitizer and antibacterial wipes with me, so that my children are less likely to contract a fatal disease.*

Peter identifies his most frequently used avoidance and safety-seeking behaviours as:

1. *Avoiding reading books about death or non-existence.*
2. *Trying to avoid the topic of death when it comes up in conversation.*

Ali identifies his most frequently used avoidance and safety-seeking behaviours as:

1. *Only travelling to places if I have planned the route to the nearest medical centre.*
2. *Always wearing my smartwatch to monitor my heart rate.*
3. *Avoiding exercise which might trigger my heart palpitations.*

Sasha identifies her most frequently used avoidance and safety-seeking behaviours as:

1. *Avoiding watching films or television shows in which someone dies, particularly if it's a parent.*
2. *Avoiding thoughts of my parents dying by pushing the thoughts away or distracting myself from them.*

Julie identifies her most frequently used avoidance and safety-seeking behaviours as:

1. *Avoiding talking to my husband or children about my death, or funeral preferences.*
2. *Wearing my crucifix necklace to my medical appointments in the belief it will bring a good outcome.*

Write your most common avoidance and safety-seeking behaviours in the space below.

....

....

....

....

Reassurance seeking

Reassurance seeking is another common behaviour in death anxiety. When we feel anxious about our own safety, or that of our loved ones, it makes sense that we turn to other people to reassure us. Seeking reassurance from others helps us feel calm in the short term. But, like avoidance, it only worsens our anxiety in the long term. Excessive reassurance seeking is also a problem because the feeling of calm from that reassurance only lasts so long – our anxiety and doubts usually start to creep back in after just a few hours or days. Here are some common examples of reassurance seeking in death anxiety:

• Seeking reassurance from loved ones that they are safe and not going to die.

- Seeking reassurance that death will not happen.
- Seeking reassurance from a doctor or health professional that you or a loved one are healthy.
- Mentally replaying a conversation which you found reassuring.

Marianne identifies her most frequently used reassurance-seeking behaviours as:

1. *Asking my husband if he thinks our children are ill.*
2. *Repeatedly going to my doctor to ask for reassurance on symptoms.*

Peter identifies his most frequently used reassurance-seeking behaviours as:

1. *Looking on online forums to seek reassurance about whether not existing is truly awful.*

Ali identifies his most frequently used reassurance-seeking behaviours as:

1. *Seeking reassurance from my cardiologist that my heart palpitations are normal.*
2. *Asking friends and family whether they think I am healthy.*

Sasha identifies her most frequently used reassurance-seeking behaviours as:

1. *Calling my parents frequently to seek reassurance that they haven't had an accident.*
2. *Seeking reassurance from my parents that they will not die soon, and that they think I will cope.*

Julie identifies her most frequently used reassurance-seeking behaviours as:

1. *Constantly asking my husband whether he thinks I will go to hell.*

Take a moment to think about whether you seek reassurance related to death. Write down your examples below.

....

....

....

....

....

Checking behaviours

Another common behaviour is compulsive checking. This is usually motivated by attempts to avoid the risk or awfulness of dying. Checking can be either observable to others (e.g. checking on the internet what happens after death) or unobservable, such as checking that you perform mentally (e.g. internally reviewing your previous actions). The problem is that it may work in the short term, but it increases your doubts in the long term. Here are some of the most common examples of checking in death anxiety:

• Repeatedly checking your body (or that of a loved one) for signs of illness.

- Checking or mentally reviewing whether you touched something contaminated.
- Checking or mentally reviewing whether you did something to harm someone (e.g. whether you could have run someone over in your car without realizing).

Marianne identifies her most frequently used checking behaviours as:

1. *Checking my children's temperature regularly.*
2. *Checking myself weekly for moles or any changes in my skin.*

Peter identifies his most frequently used checking behaviours as:

1. *Internally checking whether I feel okay with the idea of non-existence.*
2. *Reviewing past experiences (such as my drug trip) and checking whether it still makes me anxious.*

Ali identifies his most frequently used checking behaviours as:

1. *Checking my smartwatch to see if my heart rate has changed.*
2. *Checking the real-time pollution levels online for my city.*

Sasha identifies her most frequently used checking behaviours as:

1. *Checking on the internet for what happens after death.*

Julie identifies her most frequently used checking behaviours as:

1. *Mentally reviewing my life to check whether I have made any mistakes or done anything immoral.*

Have you noticed any checking behaviours that you tend to engage in? Take a moment to write them down below.

....

....

....

....

....

How does death anxiety relate to different mental health conditions?

As you have now seen, death anxiety can present itself in many different ways. For one person, their fears may be expressed in the form of being excessively concerned about dying from cancer, whereas another person's fears may focus on whether there is an afterlife.

Although we think that death anxiety is a helpful term, it is not a mental health diagnosis. This is because it does not appear in either manual which outlines all the mental health conditions that currently exist (that is, the *Diagnostic and Statistical Manual of Mental Disorders* and the *International Classification of Diseases*). However, death anxiety cuts across these formal diagnoses and is significant in several of them. On the following pages we will describe some of the most common mental health conditions in which death anxiety plays a role. These are diagnoses and terms which various health professionals might use.

Keep in mind that many people fear death, despite not meeting diagnostic criteria for a mental disorder. You do not need to have a mental health condition in order to experience a fear of death. Even if you do not have a mental health condition, you may still identify with some of the descriptions below.

Health anxiety

Health anxiety (sometimes called hypochondriasis) is a very common condition occurring in about 5 per cent of the population. It consists of a preoccupation and fear of developing a serious illness. Often, people with health anxiety will repeatedly seek information on the internet and book appointments with their doctor, as they are extremely worried that something is physically wrong with them. When a test result comes back negative, this usually does not relieve the anxiety, as it would for people without health anxiety. Instead, they may worry that the test has missed something, and may seek a second opinion.

If you answer yes to the following questions, then you probably have health anxiety, but this can only be diagnosed by a health practitioner.

☐ Have you been preoccupied with or fear having or developing a serious or life-threatening illness?

☐ Have you repeatedly sought reassurance from a doctor; repeatedly checked your body for evidence of illness; spent large amounts of time searching for information about the feared illness? Or do you avoid anything to do with your health (e.g. medical appointments) because of your fear?

☐ Does your preoccupation with your health cause you great distress? Does your preoccupation interfere in areas of your life such as work or family and social life?

Health anxiety is thought to exist on a spectrum, so even if you do not fulfil all the diagnostic criteria then you may still be a person who worries excessively about your health. Health anxiety can become more common during certain periods, such as during pandemics. Often, what drives the health anxiety is a fear of dying. The health concerns that people typically worry about are life-threatening ones, such as cancer, brain aneurysms or HIV. For people with health anxiety, their fear of dying appears in the form of fixating on physical illness and desperately trying to prevent it at all costs. However, for other people with health anxiety, their worries may include things that do not relate to death anxiety. For example, some people may worry about suffering from a long-term, intractable (but not fatal) health condition, such as multiple sclerosis or dementia.

Panic disorder and agoraphobia

A panic attack is a brief episode of intense anxiety. Someone who has panic attacks may experience heart palpitations, shortness of breath, sweating, shakiness or dizziness. The onset of a panic attack is sudden and occurs within ten minutes. For someone with panic disorder, these panic attacks can happen out of the blue. Unlike health anxiety, panic disorder focuses on an *immediate* catastrophe. While health anxiety often focuses on slow, lingering illnesses such as cancer, people with panic disorder usually misinterpret their physical sensations as evidence that they are dying, suffocating, having a heart attack or going mad *right now*. For example, an ordinary symptom of anxiety such as a racing heart is interpreted as being a sign that a heart attack is imminent. This worry about a sudden heart attack naturally creates more anxiety, and the panic symptoms increase even more. People with panic disorder interpret normal physical sensations as something dangerous and life-threatening, and this can often stem from their worries about dying.

When panic attacks persist, they may lead to avoidance of

situations or activities where a person believes they may have a panic attack. For example, a person may avoid exercising because they worry that the increase in their heart rate will bring on the physical symptoms of a panic attack. They might also avoid going out to places, such as crowded shopping centres or on public transport, and may become very worried about leaving their home. When people start to avoid several places or situations out of fear of having a panic attack, or fear that they will be unable to seek help if something bad happens to them, this is called agoraphobia.

☐ Do you experience unexpected panic attacks – for example, heart palpitations, shortness of breath, sweating, shakiness or dizziness – which come on suddenly and occur within ten minutes?

☐ Have you often worried about having a panic attack?

☐ When you do have a panic attack, do you worry about having a heart attack, passing out, dying or going mad?

☐ Have you gone out of your way to avoid situations or triggers that might bring on a panic attack, especially when you are alone (such as exercise, crowded places, enclosed or open spaces)?

Specific phobias

Specific phobias that people experience across their life occur in about 5 per cent of the population. In particular, phobias are one of the most common anxiety conditions among children.

A phobia is defined by an intense fear and avoidance of specific triggers. Thus, you can have a specific phobia of death when the presentation is focused almost exclusively on the avoidance of triggers such as coffins, cemeteries, skulls or corpses.

There are many other types of phobias. Tick any which you fear:

☐ Animals (particularly, spiders, dogs, snakes or insects)

☐ Heights
☐ Flying or aeroplanes
☐ Receiving an injection
☐ Seeing blood
☐ Dentist or medical appointments
☐ Storms
☐ Water
☐ Enclosed spaces (such as elevators)
☐ Situations which may lead to choking or vomiting.

You may have noticed that nearly everything on the above list has the potential to result in death or remind us of death. This is because of our early human history. For our early human ancestors, animals, high places, storms, large bodies of water, enclosed spaces and contamination from blood could all spell death. So, humans who anxiously avoided these things were much more likely to survive and pass on their fear of these situations. You will learn more about this in the next chapter. Even phobias that seem less obvious, such as injections, also stem from fear of death when you consider our evolutionary history. Things which pierced the skin, such as spears, animal teeth, insect bites and sticks, all had the potential to kill early humans (either from infection, venom or bleeding to death). This is why the fear of things piercing our skin has stuck around in many people today, and needle phobias are very common. For some people, the focus of the specific phobia is on death itself or any reminders of death.

Obsessive compulsive disorder (OCD)

OCD is a common anxiety-related condition, affecting around 1 per cent of the population. It is characterized by the presence of obsessions and compulsions. Obsessions are recurrent intrusive thoughts, urges or images that you don't seem to be able to get rid of, no matter how hard you try, and they cause significant distress. Compulsions are actions that you take in response to an obsession and are often repeated. You might carry out compulsions which are visible (such as tapping certain patterns, repetitive behaviours or rituals, or checking behaviours), but compulsions can also be a mental act. For example, you might say a special phrase in the belief that it will prevent your partner dying, or feel compelled to repeat a song lyric, or count internally. As with obsessions, there are many types of compulsions, usually linked in some way to the obsession. Over time, they become *habitual* or done automatically (without thinking). OCD is also characterized by the avoidance of triggers of obsessions.

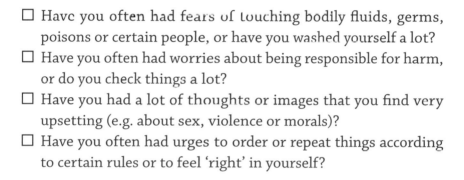

☐ Have you often had fears of touching bodily fluids, germs, poisons or certain people, or have you washed yourself a lot?

☐ Have you often had worries about being responsible for harm, or do you check things a lot?

☐ Have you had a lot of thoughts or images that you find very upsetting (e.g. about sex, violence or morals)?

☐ Have you often had urges to order or repeat things according to certain rules or to feel 'right' in yourself?

There are four main types of OCD. However, individuals with OCD do not usually fit neatly within one category and often have more than one type. The first type of OCD relates to fears of contamination by germs or bodily fluids. These obsessions are usually triggered by physical contact with things that are perceived to be contaminating or disgusting, leading the person to avoid a wide range of situations or activities. Fear of contamination is often motivated by the fear of dying or being responsible for someone else dying. For example, someone with this type of OCD may worry that they will catch HIV and may compulsively wash their hands after touching any surface they believe may be contaminated with the virus. They may also worry that their child will fall deathly ill if they fail to sterilize every surface in the home. Others may be motivated not by the fear of dying, but by trying to avoid the feeling of disgust.

The second type of obsession relates to intrusive, unacceptable thoughts or images relating, for example, to sex, violence or blasphemy. The person is compelled to mentally check whether they could act on such thoughts or their morality. Trying to correct blasphemous thoughts might sometimes be motivated by wanting to avoid going to hell. Fearing violent thoughts often comes from worries that these images will somehow bring about the death of oneself or others. For example, a person may avoid being around sharp objects, because they fear that their upsetting intrusive image of stabbing their partner means that they will act on this thought.

The third type of obsession relates to a need for order or feeling just right and having to repeat certain actions. This obsession is sometimes driven by a fear that a horrible outcome like death will happen to oneself or loved ones if things are not 'just right'.

The fourth type is particularly relevant for this book, as it relates to doubts about being responsible for harm to oneself or others. This is often linked to superstitious thinking. Harm is interpreted in its broadest sense. For example, did I make a mistake or do something wrong? Did I write something obscene in an email? Did I leave an electrical appliance on when I left the house? Could I be responsible for causing a fire? Could I have caused a road traffic accident? What if a family member will die unless I repeat this compulsion?

Sometimes people have doubts about their very existence. This is called existential OCD. This refers to the philosophical and religious doubts about your own existence that have no answers. These doubts are often quite philosophical in nature and are experienced most commonly by people who are interested in philosophy or contemplating abstract ideas.

Examples of existential obsessional doubts include: 'Why do I exist?' 'What will happen after I die?' 'Am I in a computer program like the one featured in *The Matrix*?' 'Have I left another world behind?' 'Are the people around me real?' 'What will non-existence feel like?' 'Will I end up in hell?' Alternatively, you might focus on the decisions you have made during your life. For example, 'What would have happened in my life if I had not met Sally?' (similar to the concept of the film *Sliding Doors*). This can also lead to worries about making the 'right' decision in life.

Such ideas seem very important, and you can spend hours trying to resolve these unanswerable questions. You may be mentally checking and reviewing the possible answers. This act of mentally checking or reviewing is the compulsion and is referred to as 'ruminating'. The content of these obsessions is therefore like any other obsessional doubt, which can never be answered to your satisfaction. If it can, then another doubt pops up to fill the void.

What is striking in existential OCD is how these obsessions get in the way of a person truly living in the present moment. They may be inactive, neglecting themselves, socially withdrawn and not connecting to others. Rather than trying to focus on what is in their control (e.g. working on relationships, taking part in enjoyable activities), they may be instead investing a lot of time and energy in trying to solve these existential questions, which can go on forever.

Key issues in OCD and feeling responsible for harm or death are the doubts and the need for certainty. The person usually believes 'I have to know for certain that... [I am not in a parallel world/that I will not experience the horror of non-existence, etc.].' We will discuss this in a later chapter.

Post-traumatic stress disorder (PTSD)

PTSD is a condition that affects around 4 per cent of men and around 9 per cent of women across their life. PTSD may occur after being exposed to a potentially life-threatening event, such as physical or sexual assault, a serious accident, a natural disaster or war combat. Exposure can involve either directly experiencing the trauma oneself or witnessing it first-hand. However, most people who experience a life-threatening trauma do not experience PTSD. So, having experienced such a trauma does not necessarily mean that you will have PTSD.

Have you experienced or witnessed a life-threatening event, as described above? If yes, do you have any of the following issues?

☐ Repeated, intrusive and distressing memories of the event
☐ Repeated distressing nightmares about the event
☐ Flashbacks to the event (e.g. where you feel the event is actually happening again)
☐ Intense distress when you are reminded of the event
☐ Attempts to avoid reminders of the event, such as pushing away memories of it, or avoiding places or people associated with it
☐ Strongly held negative beliefs about oneself, other people or the world since the event (e.g. 'I'm a bad person', 'No one can be trusted' or, 'The world is a very dangerous place').

Since PTSD involves being directly faced with a life-threatening event, it makes sense that death anxiety can play a role. Traumatic events often bring us face to face with our own mortality and can make us feel that our own safety is tremendously fragile. These events often change how we see the world; perhaps we once felt it to be a safe place, but we now feel that danger or death is always lingering on our doorstep. This is why freeing yourself from a fear of death can sometimes be important in addressing PTSD.

Depression

Depression is a common mental health problem that affects around one in seven people during their lifetime. Clinical depression involves a lack of enjoyment in pleasant activities, feeling low or numb for much of the time, withdrawing from other people, and feeling worthless, guilty or that life is pointless.

There are many things that contribute to depression, and fears of death (or going to hell) can sometimes play a role. A person may view life as meaningless because of the fact that it will one day end. This dread of death can drain the enjoyment out of things that once brought joy.

Depression and anxiety often overlap, and it is not uncommon for people to experience both conditions at the same time. Indeed, any of the conditions described above such as health anxiety and OCD can in the long term lead to depression.

However, if you are very depressed, and if depression is the main problem you are trying to solve, then this book may not be suitable for you. This book is designed to help people live an enjoyable life, without being troubled by anxiety about death. If you are reading this book because you want to end your life as a means of escaping your suffering, then this book is not recommended for you. We strongly recommend focusing on overcoming depression first and returning to this book only if you still experience death anxiety and once your mood has started to improve.

Freeing yourself from death anxiety

Research evidence shows that the psychological intervention most likely to help people with any of the conditions above, as well as death anxiety, is called cognitive behaviour therapy (CBT). Cognitive refers to developing an alternative understanding of the problem. This might involve examining how realistic your beliefs about death are, and how helpful they are. It might also involve changing the *meaning* you give to your worries, for example dealing differently with the fear of not knowing what will happen after death. The more extreme or catastrophic our thinking, the more intense and negative our emotional response will be. Because our brains have a 'better safe than sorry' bias, humans often jump to the worst-case scenario, often giving things a more threatening meaning than they deserve. In the case of death anxiety, people often have thoughts about death which are unhelpful or unrealistic. As you will see, your aim is to examine your thoughts, to look for a more helpful perspective you could take, and to stop engaging in any mental activity (e.g. rumination or pushing the thought away) that contributes to your anxiety.

Behaviour change in CBT refers to changing the way you *respond* to your worries. We understand that changing your behaviour is tough and requires courage. You will come across the term 'exposure and response prevention' (ERP), which involves you making a deliberate choice, for therapeutic reasons, to confront your fears and resist any compulsion or safety-seeking behaviour in the face of that fear. Another term that is used by therapists is a 'behavioural experiment'. This looks very similar to exposure because it involves doing something uncomfortable. However, a behavioural experiment is designed to test out a particular prediction or expectation. Sometimes with death anxiety, you cannot test a belief to establish whether what you fear will actually happen (e.g. it is not possible to 'test out' your beliefs about what will happen to you when you die). Instead, you could use experiments to find out whether the problem is indeed the feared prediction about death or is more likely to be a problem about dealing with *not knowing* or *not being in control*. What matters is that you learn to tolerate the feelings of anxiety ('exposure and response prevention') *and* test out your expectations ('behavioural experiments'). In this book, we will use the term 'exposure' as a shorthand to cover both these elements.

Key points

- Death anxiety refers to a fear of the death or dying of your-self or of loved ones. If your death anxiety is getting in the way of your life (e.g. if you spend a lot of time worrying about death or trying to prevent it, or by making it difficult for you to do things you would like to do), it will be worth trying to overcome this fear.
- Death anxiety can manifest in a number of different mental health conditions. However, having death anxiety does not mean that you have a mental disorder, and you do not need a formal diagnosis to experience problematic fears of death.
- Our thoughts, emotions and behaviours all play a role in death anxiety.
- Treating death anxiety using cognitive behaviour therapy involves addressing our thinking about death, as well as our behaviours which contribute to our anxiety.

CHAPTER 2

How Does Death Anxiety Develop?

Before you start the process to free yourself from death anxiety, it is important to understand what factors may have shaped your fear. Why do some people feel terrified by death, whereas others feel calm or accepting of it? To answer this question, we need to understand how our upbringing, culture and life experiences might have contributed to our attitudes to death.

Before we help you achieve an understanding of death anxiety, it is worth thinking about how our minds work in evolutionary terms. We want to acknowledge Professor Paul Gilbert for these insights.[1]

Although our brains are quite advanced compared to most other mammals, all humans could be said to have a design fault wired into their brains. There is a lot of evidence that we share a primitive, animalistic, 'old brain'. This 'old brain' is responsible for our emotions and drives, which help us to be safe, to find food and to reproduce. These drives are shared by lots of animals and would have kept us alive many years ago. We also are fortunate to have

---

1   Gilbert, P. (2010). *The Compassionate Mind*. London: Constable.

a well-developed 'new brain', which gives us much more sophisticated abilities. As its name suggests, our 'new brain' evolved much later in human history. Unlike reptiles and mammals, our new brain gives us the ability to imagine the future and think about abstract and complex ideas. For example, our new brain allows us to imagine what might happen after death, or ponder the meaning of life, unlike any other species that we know of.

The three main systems in our 'old brain' are:

1. *The threat system.* This is designed to motivate us to detect and respond to threats in our lives. When we perceive a threat, this activates our 'fight or flight' response, a system which is geared to keep us alive. We experience this fight or flight response in things like a racing heart, sweaty palms, nausea, a tight chest or shortness of breath. This system is what generates emotions like anxiety, although we might also feel anger or disgust. In death anxiety, it is the threat system that has become dominant.

2. *The drive system.* This is designed to motivate us to be interested in, and take pleasure from, obtaining resources that are important for our survival (e.g. food, sex, social approval). It enables us to survive, and also to experience pleasure. Some people try to cope with their death anxiety by keeping themselves busy and achieving things with their drive system. When this system is overwhelmed by the threat system (as often occurs), a person might feel depressed, and that they lack any drive at all.

3. *The compassion system.* This is designed to motivate us to connect with other people, and also to understand ourselves. It helps to balance out the other two systems and gives us a feeling of contentment. This system may also be overwhelmed by the threat system in death anxiety. If it is, we may struggle to self-soothe and connect with others. This is the basis of compassion-focused therapy, which was developed by Paul Gilbert and colleagues, and aims to help balance the threat and drive systems.

For now, we will focus on the threat system in death anxiety. To begin to understand anxiety, let's imagine our ancestors from thousands of years ago. Picture them living on the African savannah, at the mercy of animals, the elements and other tribes. The early humans who survived had a good threat system that kept them safe when there was a danger such as a lion in the vicinity. You will probably recognize the response they will have experienced: feelings of anxiety and panic coupled with the body automatically preparing to fight or flee. The threat system works rapidly to give the best chance of safety and survival. Its motto is 'Better safe than sorry'. There is no time to take unnecessary risks. In order to survive, you need a well-functioning threat system.

In anxiety disorders, the threats are not external (a lion, a robber, a vehicle that is out of control). Unlike our ancestors, most threats we face are internal, in our minds, and come from the 'new brain'. Remember, our new brain is well developed – we can give it credit for our ability to problem solve, plan, create language and be creative. But this is a double-edged sword. The same invaluable new brain which has enabled us to get to the moon or create a work of art, is also our Achilles' heel, because it allows us to imagine threats. So, a battle can begin between the new brain and the old brain. The new brain cannot tolerate not knowing and tries to be rational and convince the old brain that the things you fear might not come true. For example, the new brain might tell you that dying isn't as bad as you imagine it to be, or that you'll be able to cope when your mother dies. Unfortunately, as the threat system is designed to keep you safe, it tends to dominate. So, when you imagine a threat, it activates the threat system in just the same way as a real external threat would. That's why it can sometimes feel as if you have two parts to your mind – your old brain, and your rational new brain. The point is that it's not your fault – after all, you did not ask to be born a human with a tricky brain!

The key issue is that all humans need a well-functioning threat system to survive. Anxiety is a normal response, and you can't get rid of it. Nor would you want to. Anxiety might stop you running into oncoming traffic without looking or motivate you to run quickly away if you saw a rabid dog bounding towards you. Anxiety is a useful emotion for us. But often it is being activated without there being any actual threat. When this is happening, you can think of your threat system as a faulty fire alarm, which keeps sounding the alarm when there is no actual fire. The trick here is to recognize that the ever-ringing fire alarm is a mistake, and that you don't need to listen to it.

When does death anxiety start?

Fears of death are not something that people only experience as adults. Many children also experience this fear. But before we look at how children might *fear* death, let us first look at how children *understand* it.

Researchers who have interviewed children at various ages have discovered that children's understanding of death grows steadily between the ages of five and ten. First, children understand that the dead cannot come back to life. Most children have learned this by the age of five or six. Over the next four years, their understanding of death slowly grows. They begin to understand that death can only happen to living things (i.e. rocks and tables do not die), that all living things must die eventually, and that the bodies of the dead are no longer working (they cannot speak, hear or dream). As children try and understand the tricky concept that is death, it is normal for them to ask questions about it.

For many children, their natural curiosity can morph into a fear of death at quite a young age. Children as young as three have talked about being scared of death. If we look at the most common phobias that children have, we can learn even more about how prevalent fears of death are in young people. For example, here are the five most common fears among children between the ages of five and ten. Do you remember being scared of any of these when you were a child?

☐ Animals (particularly dogs, spiders and snakes)
☐ The dark
☐ Monsters
☐ Being separated from your parents
☐ Vomiting.

Each of these fears, in one way or another, may relate to death. Animals such as dogs and spiders could cause the child's death, as could the monsters or robbers that the child fears are lurking in the darkness. Even being separated from a parent can be another example of a fear of death, with children often worrying that something bad will happen to them or another person if they're not by their parent's side. Between the ages of seven to ten, children report being more scared of things to do with death (such as being hit by a car or not being able to breathe) than any other topic. Just as adults' fears of death can look quite different (as you saw in Chapter 1), the same applies to children too. One child might fear being kidnapped, another might fear drowning, but both are different examples of the same underlying terror of death.

These worries don't disappear when people reach adolescence. Fears of death and physical danger remain the most common type of fear among teenagers, more so than fears we might imagine teenagers tend to focus on, such as worrying about how other people see them. Again, the fear might *look* different, because as you reach adolescence, you are now more likely to fear falling ill than monsters or the dark, but it can have the same root cause.

Take a moment to reflect on your own life. Can you think of fears that you had as a child or teenager which might be related to death?

....

....

....

....

....

....

So, what happens in adulthood? People often worry that their fear of death will get worse in their old age. We often hear people say things like, 'If I'm terrified of death now, imagine what I'll be like when I'm 80!' But interestingly, this isn't what usually happens. In fact, people tend to get *less* anxious about death as time goes on. Studies of thousands of people have shown that older adults (such as those aged 60 and older) are actually far more comfortable with death than younger people. In fact, the elderly worry less about death than any other age group. Why might this be? It could be because, as time goes on, people experience more and more deaths of those around them, which might make death feel more normal and less terrifying. It is also possible that the health problems, pain and fatigue which are often experienced in old age make death seem like more of an escape than it typically would to younger people. Older people are also more likely to feel they have achieved more of their life goals, and death feels less shocking than a young person's life being cut off. Whatever the reason, fears of death are at their *lowest* as we approach death itself.

Born this way?

Anxiety in general often has a genetic component. This means that if you have many family members with a history of anxiety or depression, you are more likely to experience anxiety yourself too. Again, it's not your fault you were born with certain genes. It's just bad luck. However, it is important to understand what a genetic component means. Often when people think that something is 'in their genes', they may feel that it is harder to deal with that problem, or that they are destined to experience it forever. But this is simply not true. Having a family history of any mental illness *does not* mean that recovery is impossible, nor does it mean that you are destined to have the same mental illness. Being *predisposed* to anxiety does not mean that you are *guaranteed* to have it.

You can think of a genetic predisposition to mental illness as having a light switch in your brain. Simply having this genetic 'light switch' does not guarantee that it will be turned on at any point in your life. However, certain experiences in your life may trigger that light switch to be 'switched on', leading to an anxiety disorder or other mental illness.

So, although genetics (or 'nature') play a role in anxiety about death, our life experiences (or 'nurture') are equally as important, if not more. What sort of life experiences might contribute to fears of death?

Life experiences

Our life experiences can play a big role in our attitudes to death. Although experiences in adulthood can influence our fears of death, it is usually our childhood that most strongly shapes our feelings about death. Again, it's not your fault, nor is it your parents' fault – they have their own learning experiences and have inherited their own genes, for which they are not to blame either.

Let's start by looking at the role of parenting. Growing up in a household where parents or caregivers were very overprotective can shape a person's views about danger and death. For example, a child may be excessively warned not to approach dogs, eat certain foods, get dirty or do anything even remotely risky. It makes it very difficult for a child to discover that these things are actually safe, and they can grow up thinking that danger is right around the corner. Overprotective parenting can teach a child at a young age to see threat in everything and can make them much more vigilant about death and physical injury or illness. In a similar way, if a child feels safe and secure with their caregiver, they are much more likely to feel confident exploring their environment, knowing that they can return to their caregiver at any time for comfort or safety. On the other hand, children who lack a secure attachment to their caregiver, or feel that they cannot rely on their caregiver to reliably protect or comfort them, may be far more fearful about exploring the world, making fears of danger more likely.

Children also watch their caregivers closely and often mimic their behaviour. This is known as 'observational learning'. One famous experiment in the 1960s, conducted by a psychologist named Albert Bandura, is a good example of this. Bandura tested young children between the ages of three and six years old. Some of the children watched an adult hit and punch an inflatable doll (known as a 'Bobo doll'). When these children were left alone in the room with the doll, they copied what they had seen the adults do, punching and kicking it. But children who watched an adult play quietly, or ignore the doll, treated the doll differently, often ignoring it entirely. This was the first study to ever show that children imitate the behaviours they see modelled to them by adults. This explains how children who grow up with anxious parents can copy their parents' anxious behaviours. If a child grows up watching their parent excessively wash their hands, check their body for symptoms of illness, or avoid things like driving or high places, then the child may begin to do these things too.

However, having caregivers who are too relaxed about safety can also lead to anxiety about death. For example, children might grow up with parents who always leave the front door unlocked, show no concern about their children being around strangers, give them food which has not been properly washed, prepared or has expired, or don't attend to them when they are sick or unwell. If a child feels that their parents can't be relied on to keep them safe, then the child can feel that it is their responsibility to keep themselves and their family safe. This too can teach a person that they have to be constantly on the lookout for threat or danger, and that if they are not hypervigilant, death or harm could befall them.

Actual experiences of harm can also contribute to death anxiety. This could take various forms. For example, experiencing illness as a child, either through oneself or seeing a close family member fall ill, has been shown to contribute to worse fears of death in adulthood. Importantly, there doesn't always have to be a genuine risk of harm for the experience to lead to fears of death. Simply believing that death is possible could be enough to worsen this fear. For example, a child may be playing by the sea, when a wave suddenly comes and knocks them off their feet. Even if the child is surrounded by adult swimmers, a lifeguard is nearby and there is no actual risk of the child dying, *believing* that they could have drowned may be enough to lead to a greater fear of death.

Experiencing trauma, for example through abuse, witnessing or experiencing violence, fatal or near-fatal accidents such as a car crash, or war, has also been shown to lead to greater death anxiety. These sorts of experiences can severely undermine a person's feelings of safety. Traumatic experiences often communicate to the individual that the world is a dangerous and unpredictable place, with death and violence lurking right around the corner.

Lastly, experiences of loss can also contribute to death anxiety. Losing someone close to you, whether that is a childhood friend, a family member or even a pet, can bring home the reality of death at a young age. Deaths which are sudden or unexpected (such as the death of a young person, or death of a loved one from a sudden accident) are even more likely to shape a fear of death. These experiences of death can create a feeling that death is unpredictable and can strike at any time. The response of other people to loss or death can also play a role. If a family treats death as something taboo, or tries to silence any discussion of loss, this can teach a child that death is something unnatural or too terrible to speak of. It can prevent them from processing the loss or gaining an understanding of death itself. On the other hand, caregivers who excessively talk about death in negative or catastrophic ways can also make a child more anxious about death. For example, hearing phrases like 'I'll never cope now that they're dead' or, 'How can someone just die all of a sudden?' or, 'This shouldn't have happened' can communicate to a child that death is horrible, unpredictable or unnatural.

It is important to know that simply experiencing a death does not necessarily make someone more terrified of death. Teenagers who have known someone who died are *not* more fearful of death than teenagers who have yet to experience this. But someone's response to loss seems to play a bigger role in their death anxiety. People who are able to find some sense of meaning or closure after a loss often don't show big increases in their fears of death. But people who feel that the loss has shattered their views on life and the world are more likely to experience worse fears of death after the loss. For example, a person might believe that the world is a just place, and that good things happen to good people. Losing a loved one in a sudden accident can shake these beliefs, make them question their worldview and lead to a heightened fear of death. If they experience a lot of grief after the death, this also means they are more vulnerable to death anxiety than someone who experiences less grief.

So, to sum up, these are some of the early childhood experiences that can contribute to death anxiety:

- Growing up with overprotective caregivers
- Growing up with under-protective or inattentive caregivers
- Seeing caregivers model anxious behaviours
- Experiencing or witnessing physical harm (e.g. illness)
- Trauma
- Grieving a dead loved one
- Hearing people talk about death in negative or catastrophic ways
- Not hearing people talk about death at all.

However, it is not necessary to have experienced any of these to develop a fear of death. Many people experience death anxiety, despite not having had any kind of trauma, illness or major loss.

Have you experienced any of the things on the list above? How do you think it has shaped your current attitudes towards death?

....

....

....

....

....

....

How religion shapes death anxiety

The religion someone grows up in or adopts later in life is another thing that influences how someone feels about death. You might think that people who are religious are less likely to be afraid of death. Surely an atheist who thinks they are just going to decompose into nothingness must be more terrified of dying than someone who even slightly believes there could be an afterlife? Surely the more religious someone is, the less scared they are of death?

In fact, the relationship between how religious someone is and how fearful of death they are actually looks like this:

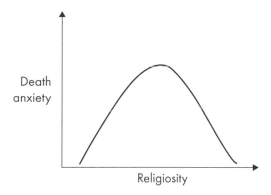

Hundreds of studies have shown that people who do not consider themselves religious at all (those on the left-hand side of the graph) are actually just as comfortable with death as people who consider themselves very religious (those on the right-hand side). Interestingly, it is people who are only slightly religious, or who aren't entirely sure whether or not there is an afterlife (those in the centre), who are the most fearful. Being strongly committed in their beliefs, rather than being undecided, seems to protect people from the fear of death. This could be because some people turn to religion specifically to overcome their high death anxiety, rather than those who either outright reject or authentically embrace religion.

Of course, this doesn't mean that a committed atheist or strong religious believer can't experience death anxiety. In fact, religious faith can bring up a whole new set of worries when it comes to death. This is particularly the case when it comes to religious teachings about morality and the afterlife. What if death brings eternal punishment? What if I go to hell when I die? What if I've been following the 'wrong' religion all my life, or worshipping the 'wrong' god? Will I be punished after death for not following the 'right' religion? Worries like these understandably make death seem a lot more terrifying.

Different religions also teach their followers different messages about death. For example, Christianity teaches that death is a gateway to heaven and an afterlife, which you will share with other loved ones. However, it also warns that hell, a place of eternal punishment, is the consequence of a sinful life. In contrast, while Judaism also believes in an afterlife, it focuses far less on any punishment or destination for souls who have sinned.

Like Christianity, Islam teaches that death is the entry to eternal paradise. As a result, in Islam, death is to be welcomed as an escape from this insignificant life on earth. However, Islam too shares much in common with the Christian idea of hell and offers a place filled with blazing fire and boiling water for those who have sinned.

Buddhism and Hinduism share a belief in reincarnation, and the immortality of the soul. Believers expect to be reborn in another form, with their 'self' living on. Buddhism, in particular, emphasizes that we should embrace impermanence in all forms, including our own mortality. In fact, every major documented religion claims that there is an afterlife of some kind. However, admission into many of these enviable afterlives depends on how you have lived your life on earth, which can trigger more uncertainty and fear about where one will go after death.

Even within one religion, the messages you encounter about death can vary dramatically depending on how orthodox the teaching is. Within Christianity, for example, the teachings about God and hell may depend not only on your denomination, but even on the particular church you happen to attend. Some priests or pastors teach their congregation that God is forgiving and compassionate, while others insist that he will punish even the slightest sins. Some teach that improper or immoral thoughts are a sure-fire ticket to hell, while others teach that it is your actions, not your thoughts, which are the true sign of your character. Further, we may also have received specific messages about God and the afterlife from people who are not religious leaders. A child's parents, relatives or schoolteachers may have driven home some strong, idiosyncratic views about God or morality, which are not actually shared by the religious leaders of their faith. It may require actually discussing these learned messages with a religious teacher to discover that the views one was raised with are not the dominant ones held by that religion. However, the narratives can be very powerful. They have been learned as a child and the emotional conditioning means that even if as an adult one 'knows' that they are not true and a way of trying to control when you were young, it still 'feels' true. In the right context, these memories or images may activate a panic attack or make you fearful of dying.

Being exposed to conflicting messages about death from your religion can also create confusion and uncertainty. And, as you learned at the start of this chapter, the human brain has evolved to look out for threat and danger. As a result, our mind tends to zero in on the negative in any given situation and overlook the positive. So, if a person encounters mixed messages about death from religious teachers, they are likely to focus on the most threatening or terrifying messages (such as those emphasizing a punitive god, or fire and brimstone), and discount the more soothing teachings (such as those which view God as compassionate or which focus on heaven instead of hell). This would naturally make someone's fear of death worse.

How culture shapes our attitude to death

On a related note, our culture also plays a big role in our attitudes to death. In many Western countries, such as the United Kingdom (UK), Australia and the United States, death is treated as something taboo, almost unnatural. More so than ever before, the dead and the dying are sectioned off from the living. People used to die in their own homes, cared for by family members. When a person died, instead of shipping their body off to a funeral parlour, their family bathed the body and prepared it for burial themselves. Death was commonplace, particularly when infant mortality was high, and before people were unaware that basic hygiene could prevent untimely death.

Fortunately, modern medicine and scientific advancements have extended our lifespans and prevented many deaths. But we no longer witness death in the way humans had done for thousands of years. Today the majority of people die in hospital and nursing homes, away from their families. People are now less likely to care for their dying loved ones at home, processing that they are dying as it happens. Even the final resting place of the dead tells us something about how cut off we are from death today. For much of human history, the dead were buried close to home. In Medieval Europe, for example, a dead relative would be buried in the local church graveyard, nestled amid the community. You would be hard-pressed to avoid a dead friend or relative while walking around your small town; your parent, aunt or child would be buried a stone's throw from your own home. But as the population of Europe skyrocketed during the industrial revolution, and the city church graveyards were overflowing with graves, people began to bury the dead outside the town. Now, visiting the dead necessitated a trip out of town, and we became even further detached from death.

There are other ways in which death is hidden from the living in the modern world. Many people will not see the body of their loved one when they have died. If they do, it is likely to be embalmed, filled with carcinogenic chemicals and preservatives, and covered in makeup. All of this tells us that death is something we should hide and pretend didn't actually happen. Heaven forbid that a dead body actually looks like a dead body. At the funeral, people in many Western countries come together in tribute to the dead person. But what about after the funeral ends? What other rituals or rites do we have to commemorate the dead? This means that people often feel at a loss for how to grieve, with no structure or cultural crutches to help guide them. Many bereaved people speak of wanting support but feeling that those around them seem scared to even talk about death. So, the bereaved are often left to pick up the pieces of their grief quietly and alone.

As you can see, in much of the West today, death is something that happens outside our field of vision and is quietly covered up. How can we expect to come to terms with something which we so rarely see? Is it any surprise that we struggle to accept death, when our culture treats it as something taboo and horrifying?

Many other cultures have a radically different approach to death, from which there is much we can learn. In many parts of the world, families continue to have an intimate involvement in the care of their dead and dying. In Islamic culture, for example, families bathe the body of their dead loved one, and personally drape it with a white cotton shroud. In several Central and South American countries, death is so normalized that it is even celebrated with dedicated festivals. In Bolivia, for example, the skull of a dead family member might be kept in an urn or shrine within the home. In Mexico each year, the Dia de los Muertos (Day of the Dead) marks the day when the spirits of the deceased are believed to return to earth. It is an occasion for visiting cemeteries and cleaning and decorating the graves of loved ones. People spend time with their family members and might even build an altar at home to commemorate and connect with a dead ancestor. Death is something which brings people together and unites communities in their shared rituals. The Obon festival in Japan is a similar occasion, where families come together to tend the graves of the dead. Japanese funeral rituals also involve a lot more intimacy with the remains of the dead than those in many Western countries. For example, after the body is cremated, family members personally pluck out their loved one's bone fragments from the pile of ashes with chopsticks. What's more, around half the population of Japan have an altar (known as a *butsudan*) to the dead in their own home. This altar is complete with photos of the dead, memorial tablets engraved with their names, and sometimes an urn filled with crematory ashes. Many Japanese people complete daily rituals at this altar to commemorate and connect to their dead ancestors, meaning that the dead have a continuing presence in their lives.

Our response to grief and loss often depends on our culture. In Japan, for example, around 90 per cent of widows report sensing the presence of their dead, often hearing their voice or feeling them nearby. Sensing the dead is seen as normal in this culture. On the other hand, in the UK, sensing or talking to a dead spouse has long been treated as a sign that you are not coping well. In many European cultures, the long-standing view is that the faster you can move on from a loss, and cut any ties to the dead, the better you are coping. As a result, only 50 per cent of British widows report sensing the presence of the dead. Their culture seems to have made this experience far less normal compared to the Japanese widows. Interestingly, modern research shows that these experiences of feeling an ongoing presence of the dead are actually associated with *better* coping, not worse. This suggests that many of our cultural messages about the 'proper' way to deal with death might actually be myths.

In some cultures, death is brought even more to the front and centre. The Torajan people of Indonesia keep the mummified corpse of their family member at home for years, dressing them, bringing them meals and chatting to them. In Madagascar, the Malagasy people reopen family tombs in the 'turning of the bones'.

The family carry the cloth-wrapped corpse above their heads, dancing through the streets. Although these rituals might seem bizarre to Western readers, perhaps the Torajan and Malagasy would find our complete detachment from death equally as odd.

While we're not suggesting that you need to dance with a corpse to overcome your fear of death, it is useful to consider how your own culture shapes your attitude towards death. In cultures where death is celebrated, or people have an intimate connection with dead loved ones, people feel far more used to death. It is harder for death to come as a terrifying shock, when you celebrate it each year, or when each day, you walk past the altar to a dead relative in your living room. When your culture keeps death at arm's length, death becomes far more difficult to grapple with.

Our culture and time also shape the sorts of worries we have about death. Some specific concerns about death were once very common but have now been replaced by different concerns. For example, 'taphephobia' refers to a very specific fear of being buried alive and dying in one's coffin. This was a common fear in previous centuries and was characterized by many checking compulsions – for example, frequently obtaining reassurance and checking over the procedure at death. In the past, people would make very detailed instructions in their wills to ensure that they were not buried alive. For example, they would request that their veins were cut or that they were buried in a coffin that could communicate to the surface by ringing a bell. Thanks to advances in modern medicine (as well as the increasing popularity of cremation), taphephobia is far less common today than it once was. Most people nowadays usually trust their doctors to correctly diagnose death.

Of course, our ever-lengthening lifespans have brought about a new range of things to worry about, that our ancestors rarely did. Diseases like cancer are now a common fear related to death, whereas in the past, most people did not live long enough to die from such a condition (or, if they did, it often went undiagnosed). So, the nature of fears of death can change a lot across time. In previous centuries dominated by religion, a fear of hell would have been more common than it is today. As secularism has increased, fearing non-existence is probably much more common than it was previously, when the vast majority of people firmly believed in an afterlife.

Now that you have learned about the different things that may contribute to death anxiety, take a moment to reflect on your own experiences. What things may have shaped your own attitudes to death, or contributed to your fear of it?

....

....

....

....

....

....

Key points

- Evolution has equipped us with a brain which is wired to look for threats, making anxiety a natural part of being human.
- Death anxiety often develops early in childhood.
- A number of things shape how we feel and think about death. These include genetics, early childhood experiences, culture and religious beliefs, and trauma.

CHAPTER 3

How Anxiety about Death is Maintained

This chapter focuses on the processes that *maintain* your anxiety about death. We will first try to highlight some of the key thinking processes that maintain your anxiety. We will then discuss the way you act.

1. Intolerance of uncertainty

At the heart of death anxiety and existential worries is the *intolerance of uncertainty*. We'd like to acknowledge Professor Mark Freeston for some of these insights.[1] Intolerance of uncertainty in death anxiety is the distress experienced in response to the as yet *unknown* aspects of death (e.g. what will happen after death or how you will die). As humans, we cope better with *known* threats or disasters. So, if you are entirely convinced that when you die you are going to go

---

1   Freeston, M. *et al.* (2020). 'Towards a model of uncertainty distress in the context of Coronavirus (COVID-19).' *The Cognitive Behaviour Therapist,* 13, E31. doi:10.1017/ S1754470X2000029X.

to heaven *and* it will all be fine, then you are probably not going to be anxious about what will happen after death. Similarly, if you are reasonably sure of how you will cope with the death of your mother, then you are also not likely to be anxious about this. The problem for many people with a fear of death is finding it hard to tolerate not knowing what will happen when they die or after they die.

Donald Rumsfeld, the USA Defence Secretary, described 'not knowing' in a news briefing about the limitations of intelligence reports for the Iraq War in 2002:[2]

> As we know, there are known knowns; these are things we know we know. We also know there are known unknowns; that is to say we know there are some things we do not know. But there are also unknown unknowns – the ones we don't know we don't know.

To unpack this, there are two dimensions of unknowns: 1) degree of awareness of events (your awareness that something exists), and 2) degree of knowledge of events (how much you know about that thing).

- 'Known knowns' are things that are known and predictable. Thus, we know for certain that we are going to die and while we are alive, we have to pay taxes. A person who can accept these knowns will probably not be reading this book. Instead, they will have quietly done the things they can to prepare for known events (e.g. make a will and prepare their tax submission).
- 'Known unknowns' are things that we are aware of but do not know whether they are going to occur. In death anxiety, the possibility that we may go to heaven or hell might be just as unsettling as the possibility there may be no life after death. So, we may have some facts about what might happen, but don't know exactly what will happen – there is ambiguity or uncertainty.

---

2   Donald Rumsfeld, Unknown Unknowns: www.youtube.com/watch?v=GiPe1OiKQuk.

- 'Unknown unknowns' are things that are so unexpected or unforeseeable that they cannot be known about in advance. Thus, on death you could get transferred to a virtual world or something completely unpredictable.
- Lastly, 'unknown knowns' were not described by Donald Rumsfeld, but this is where we know for certain that we are going to die or pay taxes. However, in this scenario a person does not want to think about it or denies it. They avoid anything to do with death.

So, the anxiety of 'not knowing' whether something bad is going to happen is often worse than the anxiety experienced when something bad does happen. When there is an intolerance of uncertainty, there is a common response of worry (trying to work out what will happen or seeking reassurance about what might happen). The motivation is trying to reduce the distress of not knowing. Sometimes it seems to work in the short term, but it then strengthens the doubt and makes you more likely to check and seek reassurance again.

Sometimes people who experience anxiety try to make their life feel safer and more predictable as part of an understandable effort to reduce their overall levels of stress. For example, you might try to prevent uncertainty in everyday life by avoiding surprises. You may like order and always follow the same routines. However, this means you may become less and less flexible and less receptive to uncertainty, which can ultimately mean more discomfort.

The less you practise tolerating doubts and not knowing, the harder you will find it to tolerate them. This means it will *decrease your ability to tolerate uncertainty* and you will find it more difficult to know whether something is true or not. It drives your anxiety up and leads you to check or seek reassurance. Sometimes the process of checking will turn up ambiguous information and increase your doubts. For example, if you have doubts about what will happen after death, you might keep checking on websites and forums and seeking reassurance from friends or a religious authority. Not surprisingly, you will receive conflicting or ambiguous information (as it's not known) and this will just fuel your doubts and anxiety.

Sometimes, when intolerance of uncertainty is high, you may become paralysed and avoid making a decision, or not turn up to an event to reduce the feeling of uncertainty. However, *not* making a decision is also a decision, which has consequences. Consider the story of the camel in the desert: a camel is deep in a hot and dry desert. She is severely dehydrated and knows that if she doesn't drink very soon, she will surely die. She arrives at a fork in the path. The camel knows that at the end of one path there is fresh, cool, drinking water in a well, and at the end of the other well there is some dirty water. If she drinks the dirty water, she may get ill for a few days but will very likely survive. However, she does not know which well is which. Because she cannot bear the feeling of not knowing and wants to be 100 per cent certain that she does not drink the dirty water, she is unable to take the risk. That, of course, is the end of the camel as she shrivels up and dies in the desert. Thus, not making a decision (and taking a risk) is a decision and has unintended consequences. In death anxiety, you may be avoiding making any decisions about death and trying not to think about it. This has consequences.

Can you identify examples of how you find it difficult to tolerate uncertainty in relation to death?

....

....

....

....

How does this then impact your behaviour? For example, do you seek reassurance, check or avoid situations or make a decision in order to prevent feeling uncertain?

....

....

....

....

....

2. Magical thinking

Magical thinking, or superstitious thinking, refers to the belief that you have the power to influence certain outcomes or situations which are actually out of your control. Superstitious thinking can sometimes relate to culture, and what people have been taught by those around them. For example, a religious tradition might teach that carrying certain objects (like holy medallions or crucifixes) will prevent bad things from happening to you. One example of magical thinking would be the idea that repeating certain phrases to yourself can prevent a car accident from happening to a family member, even though there is no connection between your action (repeating the phrase) and the outcome (someone having a car accident). It's as if you have a god-like power to cause or prevent death from happening. This sense of responsibility can lead to *excessive* efforts to ensure that the bad event is not going to happen.

Can you identify examples of the ways you have magical thinking in relation to death?

....

....

....

....

....

How does this lead you to change your behaviour?

....

....

....

....

3. Catastrophizing

Catastrophizing refers to the tendency to overestimate the degree of threat (catastrophize) and underestimate your or your loved one's ability to cope or seek help. Common examples of catastrophizing in death anxiety are beliefs like, 'If I died suddenly, my partner wouldn't be able to cope, and our children would end up in care' or, 'If my loved one has a temperature, they must be fatally ill.' Others have more specific beliefs like, 'I'll get AIDS and then I'll pass it on to my partner and we'll both die.' Often, as your anxiety increases, you use this building anxiety as evidence that something catastrophic will happen unless you do something to stop it. You might also misinterpret the signs of anxiety, such as dizziness, as evidence that you are losing control and will die, which will further increase your anxiety. This, in turn, feeds the obsession and anxiety and you have set up another vicious circle.

There is also a tendency to *overgeneralize*. This means you apply one experience and generalize it to all experiences, including those in the future. Thus, if you once found a lump in your body and believed it was a threat to your life, you are now constantly on the alert for more lumps. Or, because you once witnessed or heard about someone having a painful death, you believe that all deaths will be like this.

Can you identify examples of the ways you catastrophize in relation to death?

....

....

....

....

....

How does this lead you to change your behaviour?

··

··

··

··

··

4. Emotional reasoning

Emotional reasoning occurs when you use *feeling* anxious as evidence that there is a threat. For example, you might start to feel your heart racing or experience a whole range of sensations like feeling sweaty, shaky, sick, dizzy or short of breath. Not everyone has all these feelings, but they are a normal response to believing that an imminent catastrophe will threaten you or others. There is no external threat, but you think there is because of feeling anxious. For example, someone might say, 'Death *feels* terrifying, so it must be an awful experience' or, 'I *feel* like I wouldn't cope with my father's death, so I probably won't.'

Can you identify examples of emotional reasoning in relation to death?

....

....

....

....

....

How does this lead you to change your behaviour?

....

....

....

....

....

5. 'Awfulizing'

The process of 'awfulizing' means tending to describe something as 'awful, horrible, terrible or things couldn't be worse', and having a high need to feel comfortable. For example, on a scale of 0–100 per cent, you might rate an experience of being in a cemetery as 100 per cent awful. The problem is that such an extreme way of thinking about a cemetery only serves to make it seem more frightening. The consequence? More anxiety.

Can you identify examples of 'awfulizing' in relation to death?

....

....

....

....

....

How does this lead you to change your behaviour? For example, what do you avoid?

....

....

....

....

....

6. The importance of control

Another common belief among people with death anxiety is that they should have absolute control or influence over events (even though they know that this is impossible). Sometimes this is manifested in excessive planning around death. At one extreme, some people aim to have enough money to freeze their body (cryonics) in the hope that they will one day be resurrected. However, desperately trying to get control can cause its own problems. Trying too hard to control your thoughts is a problem which we will discuss in a later chapter.

Can you identify examples of trying to control events or thoughts of death?

....

....

....

....

Which processes are relevant for you?

We have described several thinking processes in this chapter. Which ones are most relevant to you? This is going to be important for you to be able to identify and label what you are doing with your own worries. For example, Peter identifies 'intolerance of uncertainty' and 'emotional reasoning' as being most important for his death anxiety.

Try to reflect on which processes seem relevant to your worries about death, and jot them down here.

1 ....

2 ....

3 ....

4 ....

How the way you act maintains your death anxiety

This next section is about exploring how you cope with your thoughts and feelings about death. It will focus on understanding how the solutions you have developed (such as avoidance, checking or controlling your thoughts) are contributing to your problems instead of solving them.

1. Escape and avoidance behaviour

The motivation behind avoidance is to keep you safe and prevent you feeling uncomfortable. However, when there is no actual threat, there are many unintended consequences of avoidance. Put simply, each time you escape or avoid a situation this behaviour is strengthened, because it prevents you from learning: a) that you can tolerate your anxiety, and b) whether your feared expectations do actually happen. This means you are more likely to avoid the situation or activity when the situation arises again.

For example, imagine that you are watching the news and it begins to talk about a natural disaster which has killed many people. You immediately feel a spike in your anxiety and you quickly turn off the television and walk out of the living room. What happens to your anxiety level? Now that you have 'escaped' or avoided this reminder of death, your anxiety will start to reduce. But what has really happened here? By escaping the feared situation (the news piece about death), the unpleasant symptoms of anxiety have gone away. This reduction in uncomfortable feelings is strengthened, meaning that next time you face anxiety, you will be even more likely to avoid or escape it. But, by doing so, you will never get the chance to test out your expectations (such as 'I couldn't cope with hearing about death'), and to actually practise being comfortable or accepting of the physical sensations of anxiety.

This is a very important point to understand. Avoidance may reduce our anxiety in the short term, but it worsens it in the long term. Each time you avoid or escape a feared situation (e.g. by turning away from the funeral home when you walk past it), you miss out on the chance to learn to tolerate the anxiety. Each time you change the topic when someone talks about death or turn off the film when a character is dying, you also get stuck at the worst moment and don't get to find out how it turned out, or whether there were elements of hope in the story. This completes the cycle and feeds your worry. In summary, avoidance is the problem not the solution. The unintended consequence is that it strengthens your fears and doubts about death. This is because avoidance robs you of the opportunity to learn that the thing you are fearing is not as awful as you think it is, and that you can tolerate anxiety.

Can you identify some examples of the way you avoid or escape from triggers about the thoughts of or objects related to death?

....

....

....

....

What effect does this have on your fears and doubts?

....

....

....

....

2. Thought suppression

Avoidance can also occur in your mind. You may not want to think about your own or a loved one's death. Again, the intention is to keep you safe and prevent you feeling awful. However, it only works in the short term. The unintended consequence is that it strengthens your fears and doubts about death.

To see this in action, try the following exercise:

- Close your eyes and imagine something you are ashamed of.
- Try really hard not to think about what you are ashamed of for a minute. Actively try to push any such thoughts or images out of your mind.

What did you notice was the effect of trying not to think about what you are ashamed of?

Most people find that is all they can think about. Understanding the apparent upside-down way in which the human mind works is key to understanding and freeing yourself from death anxiety. Many people with this problem are caught in the trap of trying too hard to rid themselves of such thoughts.

Of course, there are other things which temporarily get rid of thoughts and feelings: alcohol or other drugs, comfort eating, excessive gambling, hitting your head, and so on. Avoidance works in the short term but at a high cost. In the long term, it makes you feel more fearful and less confident. The avoidance mechanisms feed the worry and *become* the problem. The implication for freeing yourself from death anxiety is clear – stop trying so hard not to have the doubt, thought or image that's bothering you, and it will bother you much less! After all, a thought can't be intrusive if you don't let it bother you, and recognize it for what it is. It's just a thought and has no implications for the future.

Can you identify how you suppress any thoughts or feelings?

....

....

....

What effect does this have on your fears and doubts?

....

....

....

3. Attentional bias

Your attention is a limited resource: the more attention is directed at what you think may be dangerous and how you feel, the less attention there is for normal tasks. Being excessively focused on threats is also likely to increase your vigilance of situations that might be dangerous. If too much of your attention is taken up by scanning for danger, it will be impossible to relax or concentrate on normal activities. The process of excessive vigilance and the anticipation of danger is not specific to death anxiety, as it will occur in other anxiety disorders. For example, if you have been involved in a road traffic accident, then you are more likely to drive very cautiously and be constantly checking other road users.

If you have death anxiety, you are likely to focus your attention on situations that you think could be dangerous. This has the effect of magnifying the event and making you more aware of it.

If you have been pregnant, or have ever wanted to become pregnant, you may have noticed that suddenly the world seemed to be flooded with pregnant women and babies. How about if you have just bought a new car? Have you found that you kept noticing the same type of car on the road? It's not that more babies are being born, or more cars of the same model being bought, it's just that your attention is seeking out the subjects that interest you: it is biased towards those subjects. What is on your mind will influence what you notice; it's just part of how the human brain works.

In death anxiety, this attentional bias is one of the factors that keeps the condition going. For example, you might be more aware of hearses, funeral parlours or references to death or road traffic accidents in the media, which others have not really noticed.

What do you 'over-notice'? Take a moment to consider identifying what you tend to notice more of than the average person in the street would and how this relates to your death anxiety.

What are you over-aware of?

....

....

What effect does this have on your fears and doubts?

....

4. Safety-seeking behaviours

You recall that we previously defined a 'safety-seeking behaviour' as an action that you do because you think it will keep you safe, prevent harm or stop you experiencing anxiety. The problem is that such actions just maintain your anxiety. This is because when our feared outcome doesn't happen, we give the credit to the safety behaviour, rather than concluding that perhaps we overestimated the likelihood of the feared outcome itself.

For example, if you are anxious about your children flying, you might light a candle every time they fly. Then, each time the plane lands safely, you will conclude that it is due to the lighting of the candle, rather than the fact that the odds of a plane crashing are incredibly low. So, even though you are not directly preventing your children from flying, you will never overcome this fear, because you will always attribute their safety to the safety behaviour. It functions as a form of avoidance, because you are avoiding fully facing the fear without all of your attempts to preserve safety. The unintended consequence of the safety behaviour is that it strengthens your fears and doubts. It can also:

- lead to the false conclusion that it was the act of keeping control that prevented the feared catastrophe from happening
- prevent you from discovering that your fear won't come true or that it is not as awful as you anticipated.

A common response to intrusive thoughts, images and urges, where you are afraid that you may do something dangerous, is to try too hard to control your behaviour. For example, if you fear losing control and doing something impulsive at a train station, you might try to keep tight control of your behaviour. The unfortunate thing about this is that, apart from using up a lot of your time and energy, it focuses your attention on your body and leads you to be acutely aware of physical sensations that you otherwise would not notice. This then triggers more misinterpretations of these sensations, which appear to be evidence that you're really on the verge of losing control.

One of the worst costs of keeping tight control of behaviour is that it can lead the individual with death anxiety to conclude things like: 'I narrowly escaped dying; luckily I just managed to stay in control...this time. I'd better be extra careful next time.' There is a famous illustration of this in the 'keeping the tigers from the train' story.

A man was travelling on a train. The train guard walked past and noticed that the man was throwing crumbs of bread out of the window. The guard stopped and asked, 'Excuse me, sir, can I ask why you are throwing crumbs of bread out of the window?' The man, continuing his unusual behaviour, turned to look at the guard and said, 'To keep the tigers away from the train.' The guard, still more puzzled, responded, 'But there are no tigers here, sir.' The man replied, 'That's right; you see, it works!'

Reflect on which safety-seeking behaviours seem relevant to your anxiety about death, jot them down here and think about how they maintain your anxiety about death.

1 ....

2 ....

3 ....

Compulsions

A compulsion is a type of safety behaviour, but it is also an act that you do repeatedly. It can either be observed by others (e.g. scanning your skin for signs of cancer) or a mental act that cannot be observed (e.g. mentally reviewing your actions to check that you did not touch anything that could kill you). Mental compulsions are often complex and are sometimes referred to as 'neutralizing'. An example is saying a special phrase in the belief that it will prevent your partner dying. The point about all compulsions is that although you feel they work in the short term, they become strengthened, because you are more likely to repeat what you did next time. Compulsions are a problem because the unintended consequence is that they prevent you from tolerating the anxiety and testing out your expectations. Reassurance seeking about whether you are suffering from a serious illness is a special type of checking with another person. This is an example of where your checking leads to secondary consequences, where people might get fed up with you and are less able to provide the emotional support you need.

One of the main differences between compulsions and normal actions by individuals without death anxiety is the reasons behind the need to finish a compulsion. This is a common issue in obsessive compulsive and related disorders. Take writing a will. Someone without a compulsion finishes checking over their will when they can see that they have done what they intended. Someone with death anxiety finishes checking when they feel 'comfortable', 'certain' or 'just right'. This is the main reason why compulsions can take so long and they don't always work. Interestingly, individuals *without* OCD might use emotional criteria such as feeling comfortable when they make a major decision in their life like buying a new home or whether they will marry someone. For example, when buying a new home, you might use objective criteria such as whether you are close to shops or your place of work as well as whether you feel 'just right' in the property. It's as if someone with death anxiety and OCD is making a major decision of momentous importance many times a day. Not surprisingly, this becomes extremely stressful and time consuming.

Research has found that checking behaviour (including checking done in your mind) can overload short-term memory and increase uncertainty. So, if you want to weaken your fears, you need to stop your attempts at constantly checking for more information. An example of how the more checking you do makes you have less confidence in your memory is when contestants on the TV show *Who Wants to Be a Millionaire?* are invited regularly to check their answer ('Are you absolutely sure?') to decrease their confidence and increase the tension. Research has shown that checking *increases* the sense of responsibility and uncertainty. The solution – checking – makes things worse. In summary, there is very rarely any need to carry out 'one check' or a 'quick check'. Fast compulsions are still compulsions. Do you really think you'd check if you didn't have death anxiety? Checking 'just to be on the safe side' is one of the most seductive and hazardous routes to keeping your death anxiety going.

Try to reflect on what it is that tells you when it's okay to stop a check and whether this is problematic.

1 ....

2 ....

Putting it all together

We have argued that the key to overcoming your death anxiety is to identify the factors that are maintaining it and put a stop to them. The more you can understand the *processes* behind your death anxiety, the better you'll be able to overcome it. This is a critical point: the way you've interpreted thoughts about death and the solutions you've applied may well have become part of the problem. Remember that thoughts, doubts and images about death are entirely normal. If you view thoughts as the problem, then it would be logical for you to try to solve your anxiety by attempting to get rid of them or to control them. This raises an important point – your brain is almost always trying to help, to try and keep you safe, it's just that it may not fully realize the effect.

The vicious flower diagram is a tool used in cognitive behaviour therapy to work out what is keeping a problem going (e.g. how the ways you cope are, in the long term, strengthening your fears). You can use it to help understand how your death anxiety is maintained. The key is to understand the motivation of your behaviour and to consider the 'unintended consequence'. For example, checking has the intention of getting more information about a threat and being more certain, but feeds the doubts and lack of confidence.

One of the things that's useful about writing down your own vicious flower is that it will help you understand how your own death anxiety is maintained.

Building a vicious flower

The vicious flower is a way of combining a series of vicious circles to build a fuller picture of how your death anxiety works.

Here are the steps to building one:

1. Pick a recent, good example of your death anxiety being triggered.
2. Note the main thinking process (e.g. not knowing) that was triggered.
3. In the centre of the flower put the following:
   - What the intrusive thought meant to you
   - Any images or memories that are associated
   - Any physical sensations
   - The emotion(s) (e.g. anxiety, guilt, anger) that you felt.
4. Start putting 'petals' on your flower; identify how you respond, perhaps using the following:
   - Compulsions
   - Safety-seeking behaviours
   - Mental activities
   - Avoidance behaviour
   - Changes in attention focus
   - Reassurance seeking.
5. The next step is to close the loop with a comment on how that

'petal' on the flower might be feeding back in and contributing to the maintenance of the problem. Ask yourself, 'What is the effect of... (e.g. checking, avoiding)?'

6. For each petal, start to think of ideas of how you could make things different and start to test them out.

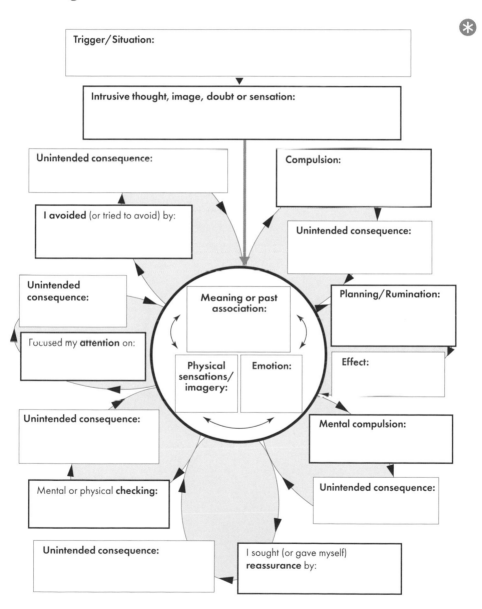

Below is an example of a vicious flower from Peter, whose worries about death began after a psychedelic drug experience in which he felt that he was dying. Note that the centre of the flower is an automatic process and is built on various associations. The petals are how he copes and feeds the problem.

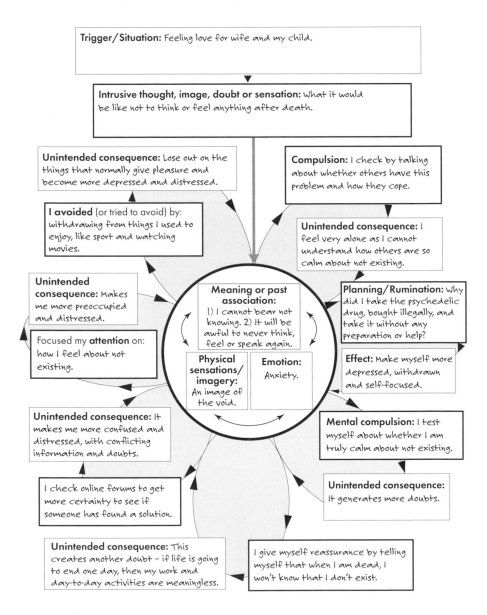

Key points

- There are several mental processes, especially a need for certainty, that are important in death anxiety but also shared with other anxiety problems.
- Learning to normalize your worries about death, to detach from them and allow them to take care of themselves, without trying to analyse, control or resist them, is a core element in freeing yourself from death anxiety.
- Avoidance and escape are common ways of coping with anxiety and keep the problem going.
- Compulsions to get more information or check your or others' safety maintain the problem and strengthen your sense of uncertainty.

CHAPTER 4

Defining the Problem and Setting Your Goals

Freeing yourself from death anxiety will be a journey. The first step on that journey involves identifying your problems and setting some goals. Once you have done that, you can start moving towards your ultimate goal of freeing yourself from death anxiety and reclaiming your life. This involves setting up two competing theories on how to understand the problem. In this chapter, we're going to focus on what you would most like to be different in your life; that is, the goals, based on the current problems you're experiencing. We will then discuss the two competing theories. So, let's start by defining your problems and your goals.

Defining the problem and setting your goals

Without an accurate definition of a problem, any attempt to solve it is likely to fail. Why? Because 'solutions' which are developed to deal with poorly understood problems can themselves start to cause problems. But defining our problem accurately can be harder than it may first appear.

You may recall that Ali worries about his physical health, particularly his heart arrhythmia. He first defines his problem as:

'When I have heart palpitations, I believe I'm having a heart attack and will die.'

So, Ali decides on a solution:

'I must try hard not to experience any heart palpitations, and to always be near medical help in case I do die.'

Since it's very hard to control one's own heartbeats, Ali starts *avoiding* situations, such as exercising, and compulsively seeks reassurance from his doctor to protect him from the anxiety. But the physical symptoms do not go away. As a result, Ali's anxiety has got worse and worse. Let's imagine that Ali instead defines his problem more accurately:

'My problem is that I believe I will die from a heart attack, and that it would be awful to die.'

He has already learned in therapy to try to make his heart race to prove he will not have a heart attack, but has a lingering doubt that if it is not his heart, then it will be something else that will mean he will die young. He will now be able to work out an appropriate solution and goal:

'To fully embrace life now and to give up my surveillance mechanism.'

Thus, freeing yourself from death anxiety begins with two distinct steps:

1. Defining your problem, which includes:
   - a description of your thoughts, beliefs or images (e.g. beliefs about how likely death is to happen to you or your loved ones, or how bad it would be if it did happen)
   - how you *act* in response to these thoughts (e.g. the avoidance, compulsions, reassurance seeking and safety behaviours that you use).
2. A description of your goal, which includes changing the way that you behave or respond to these experiences, so that you no longer behave in ways that restrict your life (e.g. tolerating physical symptoms or intrusive thoughts, stopping reassurance seeking, or no longer avoiding) and are focused on living life to the full despite your fears and doubts.

Once you have undertaken these steps, you can start to move from where you are now (your problem) to where you want to be (your goal). Each step you take towards accepting death, and viewing it as something natural and universal, will help to reduce both your feelings of anxiety and the frequency of your worries or anxious behaviours.

Defining your problem

Let's look at Sasha for an example of how to define problems. Sasha defines and rates her problems as follows:

1. *Feeling extremely anxious about my intrusive images of my parents dying. I try to distract myself when these thoughts pop into my mind.*
2. *Feeling compelled to check in on my parents, and being unable to enjoy any time spent alone in case something bad has happened to them.*

3. *Avoiding watching any movies or television shows where someone dies, especially if this person is a family member of a main character.*

Take a moment now to jot down a few problems of your own in the table below, using Sasha's example as a guide.

Rating the severity of your problems

Once you have defined your own problems regarding death anxiety, it is useful to rate the severity of each of these. Rating the severity of your death anxiety now and later will help you to monitor your progress and notice any improvements you may have achieved. We recommend rating these weekly, so that you can monitor your progress regularly.

Using the table below, rate the severity of each problem from 0 to 10, where 0 = no distress/no loss of ability to function, and 10 = extreme distress/inability to function in almost any area of life.

Problem 1	Rating

Problem 2	Rating

Setting your goals: some general guidelines

Goals are a central part to freeing yourself from death anxiety. They are especially important when you are undergoing a self-guided treatment. This is because it is up to you to measure your own progress and determine what parts of treatment have been effective for you. It is important to measure your progress towards these goals regularly.

So, make sure you have written down and rated your problems and goals before you move any further through this programme.

When she thinks about her three problems, Sasha realizes she has three general, overall goals that she wants to work towards throughout treatment:

1. To fully accept her thoughts about her parents dying
2. To no longer act on her urges to check in on her parents
3. To be able to tolerate movies or television shows which featured death.

Although Sasha thinks these goals are important, they are also a bit vague. How could she measure them, or know when she had reached them?

This is a common problem when setting goals. To overcome this, and to make your goal setting as effective as possible, try to create a SMART goal. Ask yourself the following questions to see whether your goal is SMART:

- Is it **S**pecific?
- Is it **M**easurable?
- Is it **A**chievable?
- Is it **R**elevant to your problem?
- Is it **T**ime bound (has to be done by a particular time)?

First, try to make your goal as specific and objective as possible. This way, you can easily know when you have made progress towards your goal.

So a **S**pecific goal for someone who is anxious about dying from cancer might be: 'To check my breasts for signs of cancer just once in the next month, for just five minutes.'

This is a good example of a SMART goal because it is **M**easurable (it has a clear cut-off point of five minutes once a month), and it is **A**chievable to finish within 15 minutes. It is **R**elevant to the person's problem, as the frequent and lengthy time spent checking her body for cancer is getting in the way of her achieving her goals. It is also **T**ime bound, because the goal was to achieve this within the next month. This is much more effective than setting a non-specific goal such as, 'To check my body a normal amount', which is quite vague.

Here are some examples of SMART goals from the characters we introduced in Chapter 1.

Marianne: 1) Within the next month, to leave my children with a family member for one day, without phoning them for reassurance and to check that they are okay. 2) Within a month, to write a guardianship document in terms of who I wish to care for my children if I and my partner die.

Peter: This week, to resist the urge to check online forums about death each day and instead seek emotional support from my partner without discussing the topic.

Ali: 1) Within two weeks, to go for a ten-minute jog without monitoring my heart rate. 2) Within three months, to write my will.

Sasha: 1) Within the next two weeks, to watch a movie in which family members die, without pushing away thoughts of my own parents. 2) Within four weeks, to seek emotional support from my parents when I am feeling anxious but not discuss whether they are physically safe.

Julie: In the next week, to spend one hour researching different funeral arrangements in my local area and discuss them with my partner.

Now, think of one of your own problems that you wrote down earlier. Next, think of a SMART goal that you could aim for. Remember to add to and revise your goals, especially after you have read Chapter 7 on tasks to be done before death. A sheet for recording your goals is also provided later in this chapter.

Organize your goals

Now it's time to organize your goals. Here are a few tips to get you started:

- *Prioritize your goals.* A general rule of thumb is to start with the goal that is easiest to tackle. For this purpose, place your goals in order of difficulty. Alternatively, you could also start with the goal that is causing the most interference in your life.
- *Give yourself a timetable.* Set yourself a realistic date by which you plan to move on to the next goal. It can be helpful to have goals for the short term (achievable in the next week or so), medium (next few months) and long term (reasonably be achieved within the next six months to a year).
- *Break down each goal into individual tasks.* Breaking down one goal into smaller, concrete tasks can help make the goal feel more achievable and increase your odds of success. For each goal, plan a series of tasks that will help you reach that goal. For example, this may include specific exposure exercises. As you did with your goals in step 1, you can order these tasks in a hierarchy of difficulty too. This way, you can begin with easier tasks and work your way up to more difficult tasks.

Make your goals realistic

It is important to make sure our goals are realistic, to increase our chances of success. Sometimes, people with anxiety may have forgotten what is normal, or how most other people respond to thoughts or urges. For example, they may not be sure how often most people seek medical advice on a new physical symptom. There are a few good ways of finding out what is 'normal':

- Try to revert to how you used to behave before you developed death anxiety.
- Ask friends or family members what they do. Be mindful of who you ask! Asking people you view as rational and calm will be more helpful than asking people who are very anxious themselves.
- Where relevant, seek information online from health organizations (e.g. for recommendations on how to prepare for death, or how often to perform self-examinations for various illnesses).

To help you get started setting realistic and achievable goals, we will give a brief overview of some suitable goals for some common problem behaviours. Even if your own problems aren't specifically covered here, this should help you get the general idea of how to tailor your goals to your own individual behaviours.

If you are struggling to identify goals, read Chapter 7 for tasks to do for death anxiety.

If you typically avoid reminders of death, or thoughts, situations or places to do with death, it can be helpful to consider goals to overcome these. Some example goals include:

- *'To be able to watch a film where the main character dies.'*
- *'To sit down with my partner for an hour and discuss our funeral wishes.'*
- *'To be able to visit a hospital.'*

- *'To be able to walk through my local cemetery.'*

As you can see, each of these goals is very specific to death. However, you might do a range of other anxious behaviours as a means of preventing death. Below, we have included some more information on appropriate goals for other conditions which may stem from death anxiety.

Example goals

A common problem for people with health anxiety is knowing when is appropriate to seek medical attention. A good rule of thumb is the 'wait for two weeks' approach. Usually, most symptoms will disappear naturally after two weeks, even without any medical intervention. If after two weeks the symptom is still persisting, it is reasonable to see a doctor for advice. If you have a high fever, intense pain or signs of worsening infection, it is reasonable to seek medical attention promptly.

People with health anxiety also often research their symptoms online, even though no internet search can confirm whether you have a condition or provide any conclusive answer. As a result, the goal should be to not research symptoms online at all. Another common problem is knowing how often to perform self-examinations for serious illnesses. The most effective approach here is to follow the advice of respected health organizations. Some example goals are as follows:

- *'I will check my body for signs of skin cancer just once every three months, for 15 minutes each time, as per the medical recommendations.'*
- *'I will self-examine for lumps on my breasts just once each month, as the Breast Cancer charity recommends.'*
- *'When I have a headache, I will manage it with standard pain relief.'*

If the headaches are persisting for more than two weeks, I will make an appointment to see my doctor.'

We know that excessive checking on the internet for more information about something that is unknown just creates more uncertainty. If you must check, use only a reliable site that tells you what to do (e.g. a government website on what to do in a pandemic). So the goal may be a brief check every two weeks to see if the advice has altered.

Goal sheet

Now, write your goals in the table below. Next, rate how close you are to achieving each of your goals on a scale between 0 and 10, where 0 = no progress whatsoever and 10 = goal achieved and sustained constantly.

Goal 1	Rating

Goal 2	Rating

Building a competing explanation: Theory A/Theory B

One aspect of freeing yourself from death anxiety is to gather evidence to see 'which theory fits the facts'. An approach called

Theory A/Theory B, developed by Professor Paul Salkovskis[1] and often used in CBT for health anxiety or OCD, can help. For this, you will need to think of Theory A as your current feared consequence. Theory B is the view that your problem is *not* the risk or awfulness of what you most fear, but your worry and doubt itself. For example, imagine you have a fear about what will happen after death:

Theory A: It is truly awful to not know what will happen after death.

- If Theory A is true, then I must get as much information as possible to know what will happen after death.
- If this theory is true, then what this says about the future is that my life will be miserable as I get more and more conflicting or ambiguous information.

Theory B: My problem is my excessive *worrying and having doubts* about not knowing what will happen after death.

- If Theory B is true, then I have to act against this worry and doubt by deliberately embracing my fear, stopping getting more information and tolerating not knowing.
- If this is true, then what this says about the future is that my worry and doubts will reduce and I can enjoy life again.

You may not be 100 per cent sure whether Theory A or Theory B is true, which is completely normal. Here is where your courage and compassion will help. Choose a warmer, less-judgemental perspective, use courage to live with the uncertainty and see how this alternative works in practice.

---

1   Salkovskis, P.M. and Kirk, J. (2007). 'Obsessional Disorders.' In K. Hawton, P.M. Salkovskis, J. Kirk, *et al.* (eds) *Cognitive Behaviour Therapy for Psychiatric Problems: A Practical Guide*, pp.129–168. Oxford: Oxford University Press.

Identifying your own Theory A or Theory B

Try thinking of your own main worries in terms of two competing theories. In the space below, write against 'Theory A' the belief that makes you most fearful, and because of which you perform checking or avoidance and safety behaviours. Then write against 'Theory B' another way of looking at this belief that would show your Theory A to be unfounded.

Theory A:

....

If Theory A is true, then I have to act by:

....

If Theory A is true, then what does this say about the future?

....

Theory B:

....

If Theory B is true, then I have to act by:

....

If Theory B is true, then what does this say about the future?

....

Testing whether your symptoms best match Theory A or Theory B is the cornerstone of CBT.

If you have death anxiety, you will probably have been following Theory A for many years. However, to determine whether Theory B might be the more helpful understanding for your problems, you will have to act *as if Theory B is* correct (even if you don't believe it) while you collect the evidence. If after, say, three months, you remain unconvinced, you can always go back to Theory A and carry on with your current solutions.

Key points

- Freeing yourself from death anxiety starts by defining the problem you want to solve.
- It's important then to make SMART (Specific, Measurable, Achievable, Relevant and Time bound) goals of what you are trying to achieve.
- Lastly, set up two competing theories to test whether the evidence best fits one of them and act as if Theory B is true even if you don't yet believe it.

CHAPTER 5

Developing Alternative Ways of Thinking about Death

In Chapter 1, you identified some of the key thoughts which contribute to your death anxiety. In Chapter 3, we introduced some of the key processes that are important in maintaining your death anxiety. It may be worth re-reading the task in Chapter 3 about identifying which thinking processes (magical thinking or intolerance of uncertainty) are most relevant for you, and selecting parts which fit best to your understanding of yourself. In this chapter, we develop this theme further, and focus on a more helpful way of thinking about some of these problems.

As we have seen, a central skill in CBT is challenging and questioning our thoughts to help us develop an alternative perspective on a situation. To do this, we need to look at the evidence for or against our thoughts, to identify if we are using an unhelpful thinking style (e.g. catastrophizing, emotional reasoning), and to ask how helpful our thoughts are. Remember, thoughts are not facts. We do not need to just accept that they must be true. Often, our anxious thoughts are either unhelpful or unrealistic. Instead of being wedded to our thoughts, we want to be able to hold them under a magnifying glass and investigate them. Doing this will also help us change our behaviour (which you will read more about in the next chapter).

Let's consider some general worries which you may have about death and try and take a different perspective. Your worries about death probably fall into one (or more) of these various themes below. As you will see, some of these themes will overlap.

1. Thoughts about the awfulness of not existing, including how bad it would be to not experience anything ever again

This is a very common thought in death anxiety. One problem here is that, as Freud observed, we cannot imagine our own death, because whenever we attempt to do so, we think of ourselves as still present as spectators. But let's try and evaluate this thought. Is it really true that it would be awful to not experience anything ever again? In a sense, we have already experienced non-existence before. Being dead is the same state of non-existence that we experienced before we were alive. We have no knowledge of our existence before we were conceived. The ancient Stoic philosophers of Greece and Rome referred to this as the 'symmetry' argument. The philosopher Seneca once wrote to a bereaved woman: '[death] returns us to that peace in which we reposed before we were born. If someone pities the dead, let him also pity those not yet born'. In another letter, Seneca writes: 'Wouldn't a man seem to you the greatest of all fools, if he wept because for a thousand years previously, he had not been alive?' Seneca's point is tremendously valuable. For thousands and thousands of years, you did not think, feel or experience anything. And yet, you are probably not very troubled by this idea. So why should you let the idea of non-existence after death be so distressing?

Remember, after death you will not be able to think about the awfulness of not experiencing anything again or not being able to tick off certain goals. There will be no *you* to feel sad about missing out on existing or experiences you might have had. Although right now you feel that this will be horrible, you feel this way because you are conscious and alive. After death, it will not be possible to feel this way.

Another question to consider here is: Am I worrying about something that is outside my control? If so, what's the point of this worry? You would probably agree that you have no control over whether or not you will experience non-existence after you die. If this is out of your control, your worries about it will not achieve anything. So, it's not a problem that can be solved or made better in some way. The best thing to do is to live your life to the full now. If you are worried about no longer existing, you might also find the idea of rippling (discussed in Chapter 8) helpful.

Think of some times when you have already experienced 'non-existence', such as when you are asleep each night, when you have gone under general anaesthetic or before you were born. What was it like? Was it as awful as you imagine non-existence after death to be?

....

....

....

....

....

2. Thoughts about your own death negatively impacting loved ones

Like in the last example, let's try and examine whether these kinds of thoughts are really realistic. What is the most likely impact that your death will have on your loved ones? We suspect that your loved ones will be upset, but that they will eventually adapt to the circumstances and it will not destroy them. It is important to look at the evidence against our anxious thoughts. For example, what is the evidence against beliefs like, 'My death will destroy my loved ones'? Most people do recover from the loss of even their closest loved ones. In fact, although it is common for parents with death anxiety to worry about the impact their death would have on their children, often this worry is excessive and unrealistic. Lots of people who have lost a parent at a young age have gone on to live successful, happy lives, and to achieve great things. This includes famous people like Paul McCartney, Madonna, Charlize Theron, Eddie Murphy, Thomas Jefferson, George Washington (in fact, nearly a third of all US presidents), just to name a few. It is natural for loved ones to be very distressed after our death, but there is usually no reason to assume that it would completely upend their entire lives forever.

Perhaps the best way of addressing these thoughts is to do a survey of your loved ones and ask them about what impact your death would have on them. This could involve asking them how they have reacted to deaths before, and whether they think they would eventually recover from yours. If you are a parent of a young child and you worry about the impact of your death on them, you might like to ask your partner or trusted loved ones what they would do to support your children in the case of your death.

If you are worried that your own death will destroy the lives of your loved ones, take a moment to consider the evidence against this belief. Can you collect data from a survey? Have they coped with stressful situations or losses before? Would they be the first people ever to have experienced grief, or is this something that everyone experiences in life? Who would they have around them to support them? Finally, what is an alternative, more helpful perspective from your original belief?

....

....

....

....

....

3. Thoughts about losing a loved one include thoughts about the loss itself, your ability to cope with that loss, or the dying process of a loved one

You do not know exactly how you will cope after a loved one's death, and this is partly an issue of catastrophizing and tolerating uncertainty. Although you may predict that the death of a loved one will completely destroy you, remember that this is an example of 'fortune telling' – you are making a prediction about the future, but you cannot actually see what the future will bring, or how you will respond to an event which has not happened yet.

It can be helpful to think of other situations in which you have underestimated your own coping skills. For example, are there other times in your life, even on a smaller scale, when you have expected to fall apart after some stressful event (e.g. a relationship breakup, a job loss, receiving bad news), but have actually managed to cope better than you expected?

Another useful exercise can be to consider how other people you know have responded to death. If you know someone who also lost a close person in their life, it can be helpful to think of how they coped. For example, how were they immediately after the death? Three months after? Six months after? One year after? Most people find that bereavement is a process, and that the majority of people slowly recover from the death. Remember that the human species is a very resilient one, and that we have been coping with deaths for thousands and thousands of years.

It can also be useful to identify what exactly you are fearing. What is it about the person dying that is so terrifying? It could be the idea of having to see them in pain or comfort them, of not being able to rely on them or have them to support you, or of feeling alone. Once you have identified what it is you specifically fear, try and focus on what you can actually control. For example, if you fear losing a loved one because of how dependent you are on them, what can you control in this situation? You cannot control how or when they die. But you can control what you try and do in the meantime. You might work on building up your independence, or cultivating relationships with new people, so that their death feels less catastrophic when it eventually happens. If you are seeing a therapist, it might be helpful to set up an experiment to compare your level of anxiety and worries when trying as hard as possible to control the situation, and when giving up or exercising minimal control.

Are there times when you have underestimated your own coping ability in the past? How does your worry that you will not cope with death make you feel? Is it helpful in any way, or is it just distressing?

....

....

....

....

....

4. Thoughts about needing to prevent your own death as much as possible

A common belief among people with death anxiety is that they should have absolute control or influence over events. However, attempts to prevent one's own death will always be futile. So, thoughts like, 'I should prevent death as much as possible' are incredibly unhelpful, because you are setting yourself up to fail. We cannot prevent death, and we often have only limited control over how or when we die (e.g. we can stop smoking or wear a seat belt when we drive). If you could truly ward off death through your anxious behaviour (e.g. by avoiding flying, driving, high places, germs, dogs or spiders), then we would expect people with anxiety disorders to have much longer lifespans than the general population. Surely all of these anxious behaviours are helping people keep death at bay much longer than people who are regularly driving, travelling and touching contaminating substances! In fact, the research shows that people with anxiety disorders *do not* live any longer than those without. This is important to remember, if we think that we need to prevent death at all costs. We can end up living incredibly restricted lives in an effort to 'stay safe', despite no actual benefit.

Some people have taken control to the extreme. For example, some people have signed up to cryonics facilities, to have their corpse or severed head stored at a very low temperature with the idea that one day science will resurrect them. It is complete nonsense (let alone extremely expensive) and preys on the fear of death. It gives the illusion of being in control.

You might also be trying to control your own thoughts about death. For example, you might think, 'If I think about dying, it might happen' or, 'It's dangerous/bad for me to think about death.' Trying to achieve such control over your worries simply results in an increase in unwanted thoughts or a sense that they have become even more out of control. On top of that, if you were able to choose the thoughts that enter your mind, you would lose almost entirely any originality and creative problem solving. It is also unhelpful to try and have complete control over your emotions. If you try and have total control over anxiety, for example, you are going to feel frustrated and disappointed when your anxiety inevitably arises. This might also make you feel that what you are doing is not working or might lead to thoughts like, 'I'll never get better.' But, since your emotions and thoughts are natural, and will come and go throughout your life, you need to work on fully accepting them and not having total control. It is so much easier and healthier to stop trying to control your thoughts and feelings!

Is it really possible to prevent or control death? What are the downsides of trying to do so? What are the benefits of giving up this desperate attempt to control death?

....

....

....

....

....

....

5. Thoughts about how others will view you after death and the need to be remembered

You do not know exactly how others will view you after death, and this is partly an issue of not knowing and tolerating uncertainty. The precise way you are remembered after your death is largely out of your control. And if it is out of your control, then what is the use of worrying about it or trying to influence it? All that is within your control are the actions you take in the present moment, and the decisions you make right now. For example, it might be useful to consider the impact your life will have had on your loved ones and the community (we describe the relevant concept of 'rippling' in Chapter 8). Doing things to leave your mark on those around you, such as giving back to others, or creative works, may help give you a sense of meaning. However, worrying about whether you will be remembered in the distant future is not usually helpful, given that the events after your death are not within your control.

Is it helpful to believe that you need to control how others see you after death, or is this thought just upsetting? How would your life be different if you were able to let go of this thought? For example, would you have more time and energy to actually focus on doing good deeds now, or on simply enjoying the present moment while you can?

....

....

....

....

....

6. Thoughts about the dying process being painful or awful

Some people might have worries about the dying process itself being terribly painful. Often, these thoughts have come from seeing or hearing stories about painful deaths. But, again, it is important to ask yourself how realistic your thoughts are, and what the real, objective evidence is. For example, what is the real likelihood of dying a painful death? In most modern countries, a painful death is actually not the norm, and most people do not experience a lot of pain as they die. There are two main reasons for this: first, modern medicine has developed incredible pain relief, which can eliminate a lot of the discomfort or pain people would otherwise feel as they die. The entire palliative care sector has been designed with the purpose of ensuring that people have a comfortable death. Often, when we are ruminating on particular deaths we have heard of which involved a lot of pain, these are deaths which took place a long time ago, before the medical advances we have today.

The second reason that most people do not experience a lot of discomfort as they die is because of the body's natural process of 'shutting down'. As the body begins to die, the dying person gradually loses sensations and senses, one by one. The loss of sensations, such as hunger or thirst, means that the dying person is often more comfortable than we imagine them to be. Even things which a witness might interpret as a sign of pain or discomfort, such as the sound of the 'death rattle', are actually not uncomfortable to the dying person at all (instead, this is simply a build-up of excess saliva, which poses no pain or discomfort to the dying).

Decades of research into palliative care shows us that the dying are much more at peace than we might imagine. Studies which compare healthy people's visualizations of the dying, compared to real diary entries from those at the end of life, reveal that the latter group talk much more about feelings of connection, love and peace than healthy people predict. So, if you are anxious about dying because you expect it to be painful or awful, we would encourage you to question how realistic these predictions are. Are you feeling anxious over something which is actually unlikely to happen?

Do you think your beliefs about dying are realistic, or are they exaggerated? Do you know where these beliefs have come from (e.g. hearing a story about a relative's painful death when you were a child)? What would be a new, more helpful belief about dying that you could try and work towards?

....

....

....

....

....

7. Thoughts about the awfulness of death as a whole

These thoughts are often quite broad, sweeping statements about death in general. They include thoughts like death being unfair, unnatural, untimely or otherwise bad. These global opinions about death are almost always exaggerated and unhelpful. It is important to remember that a thought like 'death is awful' is just an opinion about death, and not a fact. Many people across history have actually found the idea of death transformative, to help us keep things in perspective. For example, consider this quote by Buddhist monk Kobo-Daishi:

When you tremble with worry, contemplate the truth that all elements of this world are non-substantial and impermanent.

This quote emphasizes the idea that, when we are feeling incredibly distressed about an upcoming deadline, being late for an important event, or an argument we had with someone, remembering the impermanence of everything, including ourselves, can be very helpful. Some Buddhists will often deliberately contemplate death as a soothing reminder of how trivial most of our problems are. With this perspective, death isn't inherently awful at all, which shows us that our original belief about death being horrible is just an opinion, and not an actual fact.

The problem with this original thought is the process of 'awfulizing', which means tending to describe something as 'awful, horrible, terrible, or things couldn't be worse', and having a high need to feel comfortable. For example, on a scale of 0–100 per cent, you might rate an experience as 100 per cent awful. The problem is that such an extreme way of thinking about anxiety only serves to make it seem more frightening. The consequence? More anxiety. Instead, it's more helpful to try to keep this unpleasant experience in perspective; for example, 'Feeling anxious about dying is very unpleasant (say 90%), but not the worst thing in the world.'

Part of the common issue with these thoughts is that they take our existence for granted. When we believe that death is unfair or catastrophic, we are mistakenly assuming that we were always guaranteed life, and that life being taken away from us is therefore horrible or unfair. However, it is important to understand that the fact we are existing at all is an incredibly unlikely event. In Richard Dawkins' opening to his book *Unweaving the Rainbow*,[1] he reminds us that 'we are going to die, and that makes us the lucky ones', because 'we won the lottery of birth against all odds'. For you to exist, not only did your parents have to meet and produce the only unique sequence of DNA that could create you, but their parents had to exist and do the same, and their parents, and so on

---

1   Dawkins, R. (2006). *Unweaving the Rainbow: Science, Delusion and the Appetite for Wonder.* London: Penguin.

and so forth. In order for you to be here today, for thousands and thousands of years, your ancestors had to survive threats such as predators, starvation, conflicts and wars, be attractive enough to find a mate, healthy enough to reproduce, and live long enough to care for their offspring. If any single one of your ancestors died before having the chance to reproduce, you would never be here today. Your existence was never guaranteed; in fact, all of the odds were stacked against you being here in the first place. Death seems like a small price to pay, when many more combinations of DNA sequences never even had a chance to exist at all.

Take a moment to consider the unlikelihood of your existence, and all the many fortunate events that had to happen for you to be born. Do you know the story of how your parents or grand-parents met? If you like, you can also calculate the improbability of your own existence, by calculating the chances of your parents ever meeting in the first place (e.g. how many potential partners existed in the same city in which they met? Likely thousands, and had they picked any other mate, the precise DNA sequence that created you would never have been brought into this world), followed by their parents, and so on. Reflect on how you have 'won the lottery of birth against all odds'. Why waste that golden ticket by worrying about the inevitability of death?

....

....

....

....

....

Now you have seen how to try and take a different perspective on this particular worry about death. As you learned in the last chapter, there are also several thinking styles or processes that contribute to anxiety.

8. Intolerance of not knowing what will happen

Here the problem is not being able to tolerate not knowing what will happen in the dying process, how you will die or what will happen after death. Nobody knows and the more you try to get more information the more you will confuse and make yourself more distressed.

If you have an intolerance of uncertainty around or after death, try to follow these rules:

- Don't collect more information that is uncertain or speculation. For example, one person who was very fearful about Covid-19 watched and read everything she could find on the subject. This made her even more confused with conflicting information and speculation. This is not surprising as there are many unknowns (not to mention fake news) and lots of conflicting information. In this case, it's best to stick to the government advice that tells you *what to do* and to check for any updates once a week. When it comes to death anxiety, do not keep searching for information or views about death or symptoms. Nobody knows what exactly may happen and you will get more confused with conflicting information.
- Try to set a rule of thumb, 'If it's a doubt, it's my anxiety', to help you not engage in such thoughts. Allowing 'just one check' or neutralizing a doubt may lead to relief in the short term but just strengthens the need for another check and decreases confidence and tolerance of uncertainty. Many of your intrusive doubts are just rabbit holes, and the further you go down them

the darker and more horrible they are, and the harder they are to escape from. Try to identify the chain of events when you first become aware of such doubts, and intervene before the checking, reassurance seeking or mental reviews begin. Stick to your path of what's important in your life, tolerate not knowing what is down the rabbit hole, and therefore do not go down it!

- Prepare for things that you know are very likely or 100 per cent certain, like death and taxes. Have you made your will or discussed your funeral plans? Have you done your tax return? An analogy in the real world is that there are events that are very likely, for example, preparing for an interview that you have been invited for. Wherever possible, you would practise by rehearsing for the event in real life by doing a role play (and not in your head). Preparing for an interview by doing a role play is an action and means getting out of your head. It would be less effective if you did this in your head.

- Find healthy ways of helping your mind gain a sense that all is well and under reasonable control that do not involve your anxiety. For example, if your life is somewhat chaotic without any structure, then it is helpful to create certainty in your everyday life and what is in your control. Thus, make sure that you structure your day and have a routine of when you get up and have your meals, and do what you are avoiding in life. However, you don't over-compensate and plan with excessive preparation and over-tidiness. Thus, once you have some structure in your life, it's important to also consider changing a routine or experiment for something new in order to become attuned to the bodily sensation of uncertainty. You might start with easy tasks, for example going on a different route to work, and build up to where you go on holiday. There are games of chance that can be played that have bad luck out of the blue. What you are learning is to tolerate the distress of not knowing. Over time, this means you will learn to tolerate the doubts in your anxiety.

9. Magical thinking

Magical thinking, or superstitious thinking, refers to the belief that you have the power to influence certain outcomes or situations which are actually out of your control. Many bad events occur because of bad luck, you have the wrong genes, you're in the wrong place at the wrong time, you have no foreknowledge of the event. Your influence over bad events is therefore very limited. Magical thinking gives you the illusion of control. In other words, it makes you feel better in the short term but strengthens the superstitious thinking and makes you more likely to do it again. So, the key is when you are very anxious and using magical thinking, label the process magical thinking and refuse to engage in it. The key to overcoming it will be doing anti-superstitious tasks. We discuss this in our tasks to prepare yourself for death in Chapter 7.

10. Catastrophizing and overgeneralizing

This refers to the tendency to overestimate the degree of threat (catastrophize) and underestimate your or your loved one's ability to cope or seek help. You might also misinterpret the signs of anxiety, such as dizziness, as evidence that you are losing control and will die, which will further increase your anxiety. You may also have a tendency to overgeneralize. This means you apply one experience and generalize it to all experiences, including those in the future. When it comes to changing and testing your fears, you will need to be aware of this bias in overestimating danger or threats and underestimating your ability to cope or seek help. Your task here is to correct it by acting as if this a false signal. So, the key is when you are very anxious, identify the process of catastrophizing or overgeneralizing and refuse to engage in it. Another alternative is to consider a best-case or realistic scenario and try to dial down the catastrophizing to 50 per cent of your fear.

11. Emotional reasoning

Emotional reasoning occurs when you use feeling anxious as evidence that there is a threat. When we treat our emotions as facts, we are not able to consider whether something is actually as threatening as it feels. For example, someone might say, 'Death *feels* terrifying, so it must be an awful experience' or, 'I feel unsafe in this situation, so there must be a danger.' The problem with this emotional reasoning is that we are basing our judgements on how we feel. But our emotions are not the most objective judge of future events which haven't even happened. How often have your emotions been completely wrong about something? Again, the key is to identify the process of emotional reasoning and to remind yourself that emotions are not facts.

Key points

- This chapter has tried to start you developing an alternative way of thinking about death.
- Try to become aware of these thinking styles and practise a different way of thinking about the problem.
- Remember to use wisdom, instead of taking your thoughts at face value. Ask yourself: Is this thought realistic? Is it helpful? What would I say to a friend who was having this thought? What would a calm, rational person say in response to this thought? Am I worrying about something outside my control? Is there a more helpful, realistic perspective I could take here?

CHAPTER 6

Getting Ready to Act Against Your Fears

Exposure and behavioural experiments

This chapter prepares for the most important part of the book in the next chapter. It aims to help you have a good understanding of the theory before you start testing out your fears. 'Exposure and response prevention' is popularly described as 'facing your fears'. However, it is more nuanced than 'just facing your fears of death'. It means:

- planning to face your fears deliberately and repeatedly (this is not the same as accidentally encountering something you fear and being triggered)
- not responding to your triggers with compulsions or safety-seeking behaviours – this is the 'response prevention' part
- doing the exposure at a high enough level of anxiety and for long enough to tolerate the anxiety. This recognizes that the anxiety may not reduce when you do exposure. However, it gets easier when you repeat it again and again

- testing out your expectations. This is called a 'behavioural experiment' when you are testing your expectations (e.g. assessing whether your experience best fits with Theory A or Theory B introduced in Chapter 4).

We will refer to it overall as 'exposure' for short, rather than 'exposure and response prevention and a behavioural experiment'. However, please recognize that these are just two sides of a coin. Exposure is learning to tolerate the feelings of anxiety without a compulsion, in a planned manner. The other side of the coin is an experiment testing your expectations about the way your problem works; namely 'Do the results of the task best fit with Theory A or B' (e.g. Theory A is that your feelings of anxiety will go on for ever, and that you will lose control; Theory B is the problem is that you are *worrying* that your anxiety will go on for ever, and that you will lose control. In other words, this is a problem of fear and worry, not a problem of losing control). Some cognitive behaviour therapists will use the term exposure, and some will use behavioural experiments. It doesn't really matter as both sides of the coin are equally important.

You need to plan your programme of exposure irrespective of when your death anxiety is triggered. In exposure, you are choosing to face your fear, to trigger your doubts, images and bodily sensations *on purpose to develop a different relationship with them and the way you react to them.* Tolerating something unwelcome means getting used to it so that the strength of your reaction reduces. When you first get into a swimming pool, for example, the water can seem very cold; you soon find the temperature feels more comfortable because you have learned to tolerate it.

Being *willing* to experience feelings of anxiety is crucial. We don't want you to act as if you are on a roller coaster, clinging on to the handrail for life, gritting your teeth and desperately waiting for it to be over. We want you to develop the courage to approach uncomfortable thoughts, feelings and memories. Of course, courage does not just come out of the blue, and when you approach difficult situations, you will feel anxious. You cannot have courage and not feel anxious.

An important tool in CBT is a 'behavioural experiment', which is a way of putting a theory to the test. Just as a scientist carries out experiments to test a hypothesis, you can use experiments to learn more about the personal theories you have about your death anxiety. You will need to act for a limited time as if Theory B (the theory which states that the problem is your worry and doubts, not the actual danger of what you most fear happening) were true, and conduct behavioural experiments to test whether the evidence best fits Theory A or Theory B.

Other types of behavioural experiment can:

- improve your understanding of the nature of the problem (e.g. to see whether checking increases rather than decreases doubt about what will happen after death)
- help you gather more information about magical thinking (e.g. whether thinking about trying to make someone die increases the chance of it happening – or if it did, would it be a coincidence?)
- allow you to test out a prediction (e.g. 'If I don't get some form of reassurance about my parents not dying, I'll become more and more anxious and lose control').

We have included a form on the following page, which you can use to record your experiments.

- Look back at your Theory A and, in the first column of the form, write down what you predict would happen in a certain situation according to this theory.
- Now, in the second column, write down your experiment – that is, the situation to which you plan to expose yourself to test this theory.

- In the third column, write down what actually happened.
- In the fourth column, write down what you conclude from this experiment. Was Theory A right? Or was what happened more in line with Theory B?

Behavioural experiment

Prediction	Experiment to test whether Theory A or Theory B best explains the problem	Result	Conclusion from results of the experiment

A very large part of becoming more confident in your new way of interpreting your experience as a worry or a doubt (your 'Theory B') is to fully commit to treating the problem 'as if' you believe this. Action (including those that feel a bit risky) comes first, change in belief (and therefore change in how you feel) comes second. While you will likely need to add deliberate practice (exposure), this is an approach which can powerfully defeat death anxiety because:

- actions speak louder than words
- it avoids unhelpful overthinking and debating
- it involves tolerance of uncertainty
- it involves choosing to experience some discomfort in the spirit of achieving your desired change.

At this stage, we are inviting you to commit to acting *as if* Theory B is correct and seeing how it works out. You should find that your death anxiety improves as you finally begin to solve the problem of tolerating anxiety rather than the problem of preventing harm. This will mostly involve turning your death anxiety on its head; where you are used to avoiding, you will be facing it head on; where you use a compulsion, you will be spoiling it by doing more exposure. Acting *as if* you are dealing with (and going on to solve) a worry problem is precisely the same process as freeing yourself from death anxiety.

'Graded' exposure

Many people believe that if using exposure, you must do it gradually. They might think that too much anxiety can be harmful. This is not true. Exposure is often done in a graded manner, with a series of steps (called a 'hierarchy'), so that you face your less intimidating fears first and confront the most difficult last. But grading your exposure is just a means to an end, and new research suggests that jumping around the hierarchy in different situations is more effective than doing easy things then moving up the hierarchy in a very gradual way (doing something easy then something very slightly more difficult, and so on, could take years). Remember these key points about anxiety:

- Although feeling anxious is uncomfortable, it will not harm you. Your anxiety is a natural reaction, and a product of your 'fight or flight' system. Your body is just trying to prepare you for some kind of threat your brain is perceiving.
- If you approach your fears too gradually, you'll only reinforce the idea that anxiety is potentially harmful or should be avoided because it is too uncomfortable.
- The rationale is learning to *tolerate* anxiety. This means that high levels of fear should be maintained, because you cannot learn to tolerate it if you are at the lower levels of an anxiety hierarchy. The aim is *not* to wait until the fear reduces. This is an older view of exposure by habituation and it does not always reduce the fear.
- In dealing with death anxiety, you have to turn your thinking upside down: the more you try to avoid anxiety in the short term, the more of it you're likely to have in the long term.

With any exposure, it really is crucial that you stick with the anxiety; otherwise, you run the risk of reinforcing the idea that anxiety is harmful. Here are the key steps of exposure.

1. Develop a list of exposure tasks

A list of tasks is the basis of a step-by-step plan that you can carry out to do exposure. Ensure that you understand the rationale and purpose of the exposure. Make a list of your tasks for exposure – the things you tend to fear or avoid because they activate your fear. These may be activities, situations, substances, people, words, sounds, objects or ideas related to death. Decide when you will do the task, where you will do it, what resources you will need and how it can be repeated in different contexts. Remember that you may want to choose tasks in the next chapter that involve going over the top and doing things that some people will consider 'abnormal'.

Choose tasks which relate to what you avoid, what is driven by your values, and what involves pushing yourself into territory that others without death anxiety might avoid or consider 'abnormal'. There is more about this in the next chapter.

You can measure the amount of distress for each task by using a rating scale of 'SUDs' – Subjective Units of Distress, whereby 0 is no distress at all and 100 is overwhelming distress. In the second column of the table below, give each trigger a rating according to how much distress you'd expect to feel if you experienced that trigger and didn't perform a compulsion. Remember to grade them roughly into low, moderate or high levels of anticipated distress and *when you do the exposure, try to jump around the different levels rather than slavishly stick to the easier ones.* You may want to come back to this task after you have read the next chapter on suggested tasks related to death anxiety.

Exposure tasks

Planned exposure (object, word, place, person, situation, substance)	Anticipated distress 0–100 SUDs (Subjective Units of Distress)

cont.

127

Planned exposure (object, word, place, person, situation, substance)	Anticipated distress 0–100 SUDs (Subjective Units of Distress)

2. Face your fears

- Do not stick specifically to starting at the bottom of the hierarchy and working your way up. It is more effective to jump around and consistently focus on trying to tackle the more difficult tasks.
- Set a particular time frame, which you then keep to, like a set of instructions.
- Decide which targets you will take from the hierarchy and, for each, deliberately face your fear.
- Choose targets that are challenging but not overwhelming.
- Power through the easier targets if they are not sufficiently anxiety provoking. You may need to ask a friend to come up with suitable tasks that are more challenging.
- Ensure that the hierarchy includes things that you wouldn't normally do, or that seem bizarre (these are the anti-death anxiety tasks).
- Remember that imagining your worst fears can sometimes be a good step before doing the most appropriate exposure. However, imagined exposure is, in general, not as potent as doing

exposure in real life. If practical, it is best to follow it up with actual situations or activities that are associated with the fear.

3. Make sure exposure is challenging enough

- Always make sure that your exposure is challenging and potent, both in respect of the trigger you are facing and the time you expose yourself to it. Face your fear long enough to *tolerate* the anxiety or disgust. Exposures do not *have to be long* and sometimes quite a short exposure time may be effective. What is more important is that there is change in the level of anxiety or confirmation of an alternative understanding of the problem (Theory B). This means that there is sufficient time to be surprised and mess up Theory A. For example, when you visit a cemetery, you might feel 90 SUDs; this is understandable. You are learning to tolerate the anxiety and to test out your expectations – this means finding out whether your experience best fits with Theory A or B. The longer you stick with it the more you are learning that you can tolerate it, and that you do not lose control.
- Always tackle the processes that are contributing to your thoughts and anxiety, such as magical thinking. This 'second layer' of exposure makes the exercise more potent. Thus, if you fear that if you do something an uneven number of times then it will bring death to your loved ones, make sure you do it an uneven number of times and wish death on them.
- Don't wait for the anxiety to subside when you carry out each exposure – it will not necessarily do so, and this is helpful because you are learning to tolerate the anxiety. Your level of anxiety will tend to diminish each time you repeat the exposure.

4. Make exposure frequent enough

- Repeat the exposure tasks as often as possible in different situations.
- Aim for daily exposure as a recommended minimum until the anxiety becomes less in the same or similar situations.
- Don't leave long gaps between exposure because this allows fears to return.
- Remember that you can never do too much exposure – aim for several times a day in different activities and situations.
- Changes in anxiety within an exposure session are not really important – have elevated fears *within* the session so that it gets easier *between* each task. Always think about how you can incorporate exposure into your everyday life so that it is easier to carry it out on several occasions every day.
- Try to generalize your exposure tasks across different contexts (e.g. when alone, in unfamiliar places and at different times).

5. Don't use any anxiety-reducing strategies

Do the exposure without distraction, drugs, alcohol, compulsions, or other safety-seeking behaviours such as saying a comforting phrase to yourself or obtaining reassurance. The key is to understand the function of the activity – is it designed to reduce anxiety as this will interfere with your ability to tolerate the anxiety and test out your fears? It may be helpful *to act as if* you are not afraid even if you feel frightened.

It's helpful to 'engage fully' with the exposure compassionately:

- Use courage to approach the difficult situations that are anxiety provoking.
- Notice doubts and if there is anything new coming up that can be tested as part of Theory B.

- Practise being understanding and sympathetic towards yourself.
- Encourage yourself in a soothing, kind tone.
- Label the emotion, 'Okay, these are my feelings of anxiety.'
- Tolerate your feelings of anxiety by just doing the exposure without condemning, judging, blaming or pitying yourself or biting your tongue until you get through it. Accept that you are feeling anxious right now. This does not mean accepting that your anxiety will go on forever, it just means not judging it, fighting it, or thinking that you 'shouldn't' feel anxious.
- Do not use alcohol or medication to dampen your anxiety as this will become a safety behaviour.

If you're not sure about whether what you're doing is a safety-seeking behaviour, ask yourself what the intention of the behaviour is. If the objective is to reduce the risk of harm or to make you feel less anxious, then it is a safety-seeking behaviour and will reinforce your beliefs about being able to prevent harm. If the aim is to help you achieve your task so you can move on and do something more challenging without the behaviour, then this is enhancing your exposure and is a means towards an end.

6. Monitor your exposure tasks

- Monitor your exposure constantly, so that you can learn from how you respond, and watch your progress. This is essential whether you're working on your own or alongside a therapist. If you see a therapist, you can use this to keep them updated on how you got on with the exposure that you negotiated in the previous session. You should also monitor whether you responded with any compulsions or safety-seeking behaviours. To help you do this, we have provided a suitable form, entitled 'Exposure record sheet', which can also be downloaded from https://library.jkp.com/redeem.

Exposure task record sheet

An example of a completed sheet is shown below this first sheet.

Exposure task carried out Please write out the date and describe what you actually did.	Level of discomfort What was your level of anxiety on a scale of 0–100 at the start and when it was at its maximum?	Duration of discomfort How long did the maximum level of discomfort last for?	How did you cope? What helpful things did you do to tolerate your anxiety? Did you use any unhelpful ways of coping (e.g. any compulsions, safety behaviours or mental activity)?	Testing your expectations What did you learn about how your death anxiety works? Did your experience strengthen Theory B?	Next steps How might you progress from here (e.g. by repeating, extending or developing this exercise, or moving on to an alternative task)?
	Start: Maximum:				
	Start: Maximum:				
	Start: Maximum:				

Exposure task carried out Please write out the date and describe what you actually did.	Level of discomfort What was your level of anxiety on a scale of 0–100 at the start and when it was at its maximum?	Duration of discomfort How long did the maximum level of discomfort last for?	How did you cope? What helpful things did you do to tolerate your anxiety? Did you use any unhelpful ways of coping (e.g. any compulsions, safety behaviours or mental activity)?	Testing your expectations What did you learn about how your death anxiety works? Did your experience strengthen Theory B?	Next steps How might you progress from here (e.g. by repeating, extending or developing this exercise, or moving on to an alternative task)?
13 February I made my will.	Start: 85 Maximum: 90	30 minutes	I told myself that it's better that I control what happens to my estate than letting the government decide.	I learned that I had a problem with worrying about death rather than it is unlucky and I might die.	I will encourage others to make their will too. I can also sit down and discuss my will with my partner.
15 February A memento mori task – my partner hung a poster from the Louvre that depicts skeletons in various poses.	Start: 80 Maximum: 85	20 minutes	I tried to look away at first, but then started to laugh at how ridiculous the skeletons looked.	I learned that depictions of death are something I can cope with.	I sought out other posters that depict death in quirky ways.
16 February Watched Randy Pausch's 'Last Lecture' on the internet	Start: 70 Maximum: 80	10 minutes	I had an urge to mentally distract myself from his talk, but I forced myself to listen. I was bowled over by his attitude.	He inspired me enormously and strengthened the idea that I can cope with death.	I will try to live life to the full now.

7. Response prevention

Response prevention doesn't just mean *not* doing a compulsion, such as washing, checking or repeating, but learning to tolerate the distress and test out Theory B. We know it sounds dangerously like telling you to 'Just stop it', so we are going to discuss the various approaches to stop compulsions. (To understand this further, you might like to search online for a very funny video by Bob Newhart called 'Stop It' about the fear of being buried alive in a box.)

a. Understand your motivation for a compulsion

Ensure that you understand the motivation to carry out your compulsion. For example, is your compulsion motivated by a desire to avoid feeling anxious, and thinking you will not cope? If so, the aim is to test out your predictions in Theory B. Another way of looking at this is to understand the criteria you use to finish your checking – you might want to finish when you have achieved objective criteria, such as seeing that you have enough information, but also when it 'feels comfortable' or 'just right'. These criteria are normal when you have to make a decision which is very important, such as who to marry or where you want to buy a house. These criteria are problematic when they are routine tasks and are taking a long time to achieve. So, any compulsion needs to finish when you feel uncomfortable, not right, incomplete, imperfect or otherwise you are strengthening it and are more likely to repeat it.

b. Increase awareness of compulsions

We have previously discussed how compulsions such as checking are often done automatically. However, if you are not aware of when you carry out a compulsion, you cannot resist them. So, when they are especially frequent, monitor when you do them – for example, use a tally counter to count them. It can often be helpful to understand the chain of events or the context leading up to a compulsion. This means you can disrupt the chain earlier before you carry out a compulsion. This might mean doing an exposure task or finding a behaviour that is incompatible with the compulsion, or pointless. For example, if the urge is to check on the internet, make sure you check on a website that is the most confusing and ambiguous.

c. Increase exposure after a compulsion

If you can't resist carrying out a compulsion, then the best approach is to 'undo' or spoil it by exposure. For example:

- If you repeated an action in order to feel 'right', then make sure you bring on the obsession again and feel 'wrong'.
- If you neutralized a thought or image about death, then make sure you bring it back and always end on wishing the distressing thought or image to happen.

What not to do

Some therapists advise the following approaches (or you might have tried them). These are not recommended as they are not that effective.

a. Reduce the frequency or time spent on a compulsion

Some people are advised to reduce the frequency of their compulsions gradually (e.g. from 100 times a day to 90 a day) or the amount of time they spend on a compulsion (e.g. 4 hours to 3.5 hours). This is *not* generally recommended as it is incredibly slow and not very effective as you are not learning to tolerate the anxiety from the exposure and test out your predictions. Indeed, you may just speed up your compulsions.

b. Delay the compulsion

This means waiting for, say, ten minutes until you do the compulsion. This might then be increased to 20 minutes and so on. This is better than reducing the frequency as it is helping to tolerate the anxiety. It might sometimes be used as a means towards an end. However, it is *not* generally recommended as it does not really help you to test out your prediction in Theory B and is inefficient.

c. Increase avoidance

If you manage to resist your compulsions, do not compensate by increasing your avoidance. For example, you might check less on the internet about what happens after death but you increase your avoidance of triggers that relate to death. You have to do both: resist the compulsion (in this case by not checking what will happen after death) and do exposure, for example to triggers related to death.

Reassurance seeking

The key here is to develop an alternative behaviour to seeking or giving yourself reassurance.

Seeking or giving reassurance is a type of checking compulsion. For the loved one, just stopping giving reassurance can be fraught with problems. Here are some common ones:

- The loved one knows it is unhelpful to give reassurance but feels stuck and unable to cope. The person with death anxiety may become distressed, frustrated, angry and resentful when their loved one just stops giving reassurance.
- If a loved one just stops giving reassurance, then the questioning becomes more subtle or sneakier and the loved one is still drawn into the cycle.
- It's often impossible to stick to and so it increases the blame and shame on both the person with death anxiety and the loved one.
- Even if the loved one manages to be consistent in not responding to reassurance seeking, then the connection between the two people may become diminished. The person with death anxiety may then seek reassurance from someone else or develop more self-reassurance (which is a mental compulsion) and so the problem has not gone away.

So, the solution for the person with death anxiety seeking reassurance and to the loved one giving reassurance is to seek and give emotional support. The person with death anxiety might seek compassion and care from their loved one when they are wanting reassurance. The key is *not* to discuss the content of your worries. The loved one needs to respond naturally with compassion when the person with death anxiety is wanting reassurance. The definition of compassion is being sensitive to the person suffering and being deeply committed to relieving it. There are two sides to compassion – one is being empathic, sympathetic, caring and soothing; the other is turning towards the distress and not avoiding anxiety. It involves being non-judgemental and acting as if you have courage and wisdom.

It's important that the person with death anxiety and all the family or people who give reassurance have an agreed joint plan of action.

What it means in practice is the *person with death anxiety* being sensitive to their own suffering and instead of seeking reassurance, labelling the feeling and trying to express what they need (not what they want). They might say something like, 'I'm feeling really anxious right now.' If they can, it would help to say what might help, such as, 'Can I have a hug?' or, 'Can I have a cup of tea?' or, 'Can we go for a walk?' Note that there's no request to discuss what they are anxious about – it's similar to an exposure task, where the person with death anxiety is identifying and labelling their emotion to themselves – 'Okay, Peter, these are feelings of anxiety – this is tough, but let's try to just stick with it.' Now if the person with death anxiety can identify what they need (and it is realistic) then the loved one can respond. Equally, it is important for the person with death anxiety to not just be rational. They also need to talk to themselves in a caring and encouraging manner like their relative or friend.

Ruminations and rabbit holes

Ruminations or mental compulsions are more difficult to resist than compulsions, which are visible, like physically checking. For ruminations, you need to be clear about:

- exactly what intrusive thoughts or images provoke anxiety (which are the basis for exposure tasks)
- not linking them to trauma memories (e.g. flashbacks) as these require a different approach with a therapist
- how you respond to the thoughts (e.g. mental reviews, self-reassurance, neutralizing).

Some ruminations may be trickier – for example, those mixed with anger, shame, hurt and depression. These are too difficult to discuss in a self-help book so we will focus on the obsessional ruminations which are characterized by doubt. They are trickier because it is like going down a rabbit hole. In Lewis Carroll's *Alice's Adventures in Wonderland* the hero of the story, Alice, falls down a rabbit hole and is transported into a surreal land where nothing makes sense. It can be helpful to think of ruminations as a rabbit hole into which a person with death anxiety can fall. These rabbit holes are similarly surreal; trying to navigate questions that have no answer can be distressing, trapping a person with death anxiety in a maze. Exploring rabbit holes to find the bottom of it all can be unhelpful, sometimes dangerous.

Even if you've managed to successfully navigate your rabbit hole in the past and escaped – maybe having found a satisfactory answer to a doubt or question – was it really helpful to do so in the long term? Or was it more like scratching an itch? If, by diving into the rabbit hole you'd found a lasting solution to your death anxiety, it's unlikely you would be reading this book.

Try instead to train yourself *to be aware* of the existence of your rabbit holes but resist the temptation to fall into them. This involves focusing your attention on the world around you – not the darkness of the rabbit hole that is your mind. Being in your mind is helpful when you have an *actual* problem to solve and can be creative (e.g. how am I going to be a good parent to my children now? How can I develop a loving relationship or connect with my partner now?). So, if you are more aware of the rabbit holes in your landscape, you can either choose to go into the rabbit hole to ruminate in the darkness for hours on end – or you can choose to be in the real world and do the things in life that are important to you despite not knowing an answer to your doubts. That's okay if you choose to go down the rabbit hole, but notice what effect it has on your mood and whether it interferes in your life.

Now, look back at the 'Why' and 'What if' questions you noted in the first chapter and see if you can convert each of these abstract questions into a concrete and specific 'How' question, such as, 'How can I do the things in life that are important to me?'

Why .... ?

  • How can I..
    .... ?

If only .... ?

  • How can I..
    .... ?

What if .... ?

  • How can I..
    .... ?

If you can, it is helpful to just acknowledge your intrusive thoughts in a detached way. For example, it can be good to think about your thoughts as being like walking along the side of the road and being aware of the passing traffic, but not trying to stop or control the traffic. You can never get rid of the traffic – remember your thoughts and worries about death are normal.

In the first chapter, we described how you may be excessively self-focused. Try to practise by refocusing your attention externally on the environment and other tasks (such as really listening to someone and responding to them). Do the things in life which are important to you (despite the way you feel) and allow yourself to just experience the intrusive thoughts that you do not want. When you are ruminating, try to refocus your attention on to what you can do by your own actions. Only if there is a significant risk of an event happening (e.g. death) should you prepare for it, and then only if it involves action (e.g. preparing your will, talking to loved ones about your end-of-life preferences, or doing things which will leave behind a positive impact after you die). These are actions you can take – as opposed to ruminations that stop you getting on with life. We will discuss this further in the next chapter.

Key points

- To overcome death anxiety, it is important to practise tolerating anxiety, and to test out your expectations. This planned practice is called 'exposure' for short.
- Exposure can also involve not responding to your worries and ruminations – for example, by seeking reassurance from others, or reassuring yourself that it is 'just a thought'.
- Always try to act against the content of the thought by using exposure to test whether the findings best fit Theory A or B.
- No matter what form your death anxiety takes, there's almost always some way to deliberately face your fears. In the next chapter, we will describe some of the tasks you can do to alleviate death anxiety.

———

CHAPTER 7

Exercises to Prepare Yourself for Death

This chapter should be read after you have read about the principles of exposure and behavioural experiments in Chapter 6. Some of these tasks will need to be related to your specific problems – for example, if you are anxious about cancer, you might be avoiding going past charity shops or hospices. There are many different scenarios that can be added to your programme of exposure. This chapter deals with your specific fears of death.

You will recall that worrying about death often leads to inactivity and avoiding taking actions that would prepare you for what is likely. Death is the only guarantee in life and there are many exercises you can do to prepare for the Grim Reaper. Note that some family members or friends may have their own issues relating to death so don't be surprised if they are unenthusiastic about you doing many of these exercises. These exercises really can help with death anxiety and many are very practical.

Below, we will discuss our top 16 tasks to help you prepare yourself for death. The list begins with tasks that will probably be less anxiety provoking to most people. The tasks which are likely to cause more anxiety are towards the end of the list. However, everyone fears different things to do with death, so consider which tasks you would personally find easier or more challenging. Remember, the purpose of these tasks is to help cultivate an acceptance of death, to help you test out your theory that you will not be able to tolerate the anxiety, and also to empower you to take control of your own death. While these tasks will probably bring on some anxiety, in the long term people often find that they give them a sense of control and empowerment in the face of death. These are also tasks that can be done alone or with the support of family or friends or with a therapist.

1. Listen to role models talk about their imminent death

Seek inspirational role models who have accepted death gracefully or have used the news that they are going to die to motivate themselves to get the most from their lives in their final months. For example, Randy Pausch's 'Last Lecture' (on childhood dreams), which has been viewed more than 20 million times on YouTube, is a truly inspirational example of someone who has come to terms with the fact that he is dying from cancer and has only months to live. Neurologist Oliver Sacks spoke openly about his approaching death, after he was diagnosed with an ocular tumour.

If you have completed this task, take a moment to reflect on how it went. How did it feel to read or listen to people who are facing the end? How did it affect your own attitude to life and death?

....

....

....

....

....

2. Read books and articles about death

Reading books and news articles centred on death is another useful exposure exercise to tackle. You might start with reading about celebrity deaths, natural disasters, pandemics or articles about the dying process. One book we often recommend is *Staring at the Sun: Overcoming the Terror of Death*, by renowned therapist Irvin Yalom. While this book is specifically aimed at freeing yourself from death anxiety, any books about death are useful to read. These might include non-fiction accounts of people dealing with the loss of a loved one. *The Year of Magical Thinking*, written by Joan Didion following the death of her husband, is a particularly notable book on bereavement. A very different picture of grief comes from *Dead People Suck: A Guide for Survivors of the Newly Departed*, a laugh-out-loud guide for surviving grief, written by comedian Laurie Kilmartin after her father's death. Other books focus on first-hand accounts of being diagnosed with a terminal illness (e.g. *When Breath Becomes Air*, written by neurosurgeon Paul Kalanithi before he died of lung cancer, or *Gratitude*, a collection of essays by neurologist Oliver Sacks as he approached his death from cancer). Many fiction authors have also written on the topic of death. Leo Tolstoy's novella *The Death of Ivan Ilyich* is an excellent tale of an ordinary man coming to grips with his own mortality, as he slowly dies from an undiagnosed illness. Caitlin Doughty, an American mortician, has also written two excellent books on death: *Smoke Gets in Your Eyes*, an illuminating account of the funeral industry and Western approaches to death, and *From Here to Eternity*, which explores different cultural approaches to death across the world. Another book by Rachel Menzies: *Mortals: How the Fear of Death Shaped Human Society* explores the varied ways that death anxiety has impacted our species for thousands of years. Other books which we would recommend include books centring on Stoic approaches to death, such as *On the Shortness of Life*, a collection of writings from the Stoic philosopher Seneca. Further books are listed in the Appendix.

Which of the books mentioned here sound most useful or relevant for your exposure task? Make a plan for which book you will start with, and when you will start reading it.

....

....

....

....

....

If you completed this task, take a moment to reflect on what happened. What did you learn from reading the book(s)?

....

....

....

....

....

3. Watch films or television shows about death

There are also lots of excellent films and television shows which can be used as exposure exercises. The classic film *Blade Runner* explores impermanence beautifully through the replicant's quest for a longer life. The need to accept our own mortality is emphasized throughout the film, and Roy Batty's closing monologue before he dies delivers a powerful message on the inevitability of death. There are also lots of animated films that are worth watching, despite usually being aimed at children. For example, the film *Coco*, which takes place in Mexico around the Day of the Dead, vividly explores ongoing bonds to dead loved ones and how we can maintain our connection to them. The film *Up* also paints a moving picture of coping with the death of a loved one. The elderly widow Carl Fredricksen decides to go on an epic journey to fulfil the dream of his dead wife. The film is a powerful reminder that our lives can be fulfilling and filled with adventure, even if they don't go the way we planned.

Television shows such as *Six Feet Under*, which takes place at a family-run funeral home, are also very useful at normalizing death and presenting it as something natural. Several episodes of the show *Black Mirror* also explore mortality. For example, 'Be Right Back' depicts a woman grieving the sudden death of her partner. The episode explores the way technology is being created as a means of denying death, and how acceptance is the better option. 'San Junipero' depicts a future in which the elderly or those approaching death can choose to inhabit artificial simulations. It explores themes of euthanasia and accepting the reality of death. Again, like the other exercises here, watching these episodes and films forces us to confront and contemplate death, rather than turning away from it.

Which of the films or television shows do you think would be most useful to watch? There is a list of our favourite films in the Appendix. Are there any other films or shows about death that we have not mentioned here that you might consider watching? Make a plan for what you will watch, and when you will watch it.

....

....

....

....

....

If you have completed this task, take a moment to reflect on what happened. How did it feel to watch the television show or film? What did you learn or take away from watching it?

....

....

....

....

....

4. Collect *memento mori*

Memento mori is a Latin phrase which literally means 'remember you must die'. You can search on the internet for art, sculpture or clothing that usually includes a skull or death head. In earlier centuries, they would help remind the living of their mortality and the shortness of their life. In medieval and Victorian era Europe, they were designed to remind people to live a straight and moral life for fear of eternal punishment in hell. During these times, an actual skull would not be out of place on your desk to keep the idea of death always present in your mind.

We recently came across a story about students at Radboud University in the Netherlands who have the opportunity to book time in a grave for when they are feeling tense. They were encouraged to think about living live to the full now. This is an excellent modern take on the *memento mori*.

David has an artist friend Steve Caplin who among his many

talents creates 'curious furniture'.[1] He is honoured to look after one piece 'Puccini' in his living room which is an example of a *memento mori* (see image below). David loves animal skulls and has a small collection in his study. He also recommends a book *Diableries* by Brian May, Dennis Pellerman and Paula Fleming published by the London Stereoscopic Company. This is a series of visionary dioramas depicting life in hell in the 1860s and so it is particularly helpful if you are avoiding the thought of going to hell.

Rachel keeps a *memento mori* with her at all times, by having an image of a skull as her wallpaper on her mobile phone. She also has death-themed objects scattered throughout her home, such as small skulls carved from stone, skull-themed drinking glasses, and artworks of skulls and other symbols of mortality, such as candle flames and hourglasses (see image overleaf).

---

1   www.curieaux.com.

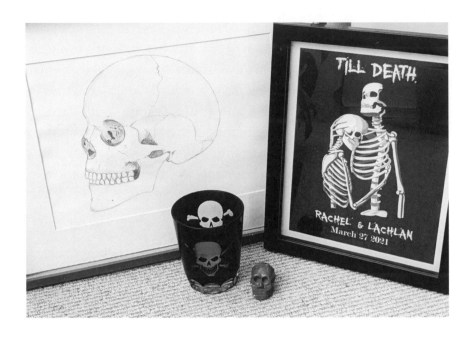

Do you have any **memento mori** already? If not, what type of objects might be useful to collect? Got any graves or body bags you could try out and reflect on what you want to do in life?

....

....

....

....

....

....

If you acquire some **memento mori** items, try and keep them somewhere where you will regularly see them. Take a moment to jot down your thoughts on whether these items have changed your attitude to death or normalized it.

....

....

....

....

5. Visit a cemetery or ossuary

Visiting places associated with death such as a cemetery or a funeral parlour are good tasks. You might start by walking or driving past a cemetery, funeral or funeral home, before building up to walking through the cemetery and reading the headstones. You might know someone who keeps the ashes of their loved one in an urn that you can view or handle. When visiting a cemetery, specifically look for headstones of people who died around the age you are now. This will help to remind you that you could die at any time, and help you build your acceptance of this idea.

Some cultures have an ossuary. This is a chest, box or building that serves as a burial place for human skeletal remains, which takes up much less space than a coffin. David remembers as a student visiting a large ossuary in Hong Kong. It had an annual ceremony to commemorate the dead ancestors that involved cleaning the graves and tomb inscriptions and polishing the bones before reburying them. He is also fortunate enough to live close to

Highgate Cemetery in north London, which he has visited occasionally and has some lovely memories. You can take a guided tour to visit many notable graves from Karl Marx to Malcolm McLaren, manager of the Sex Pistols in the East cemetery. More interesting is the catacombs of the Victorian Valhalla and beautiful statues in the West cemetery. It is all part of a beautiful nature reserve with rambling ivy. As you learned about in Chapter 2, death was much more normalized in earlier centuries, such as the Victorian era.

Rachel lives a short drive away from two famous cemeteries in Sydney: Rookwood General Cemetery, which is the largest necropolis in the Southern Hemisphere, and the beautiful Waverley Cemetery, perched atop cliffs and overlooking the beach. She has visited both cemeteries several times. Rachel also makes a point of visiting cemeteries when travelling abroad. Her current favourite is Okunoin Cemetery, which is the largest graveyard in Japan, and is nestled within a forest on the top of sacred Mount Koya. The Buddhist cemetery is shrouded in various superstitions. On a night-time tour not long ago, a monk told Rachel that if she peered into a well in the cemetery and could not see her reflection, she would die within the next few years. Fortunately, Rachel did see her reflection in the waters.

Which cemeteries would you be able to visit? Make a plan for when you could visit this cemetery, and how you would get there.

....

....

....

....

If you did visit the cemetery, how did it go? What actually happened, and what did you learn?

....

....

....

....

6. Make your will

You should make a will even if you don't have death anxiety! A will is a legal document that sets out your wishes regarding the distribution of your property and wealth after your death. It is also a document in which you can appoint guardians to look after any children or dependents and leave instructions on deactivating any social media accounts.

If you die without a will ('intestate'), then your government will decide how your inheritance is divided. Furthermore, your heirs will have to spend time, money and emotional energy to settle your affairs. For example, if you live in England, then your husband or wife gets all of the estate if it's worth less than £270,000. If it is worth more than this, the husband or wife gets half of the estate. The other half is then divided equally between the surviving children. Even if this outcome would not bother you, the *process* of making your will is helpful for overcoming your death anxiety.

The process of making a will varies depending on where you live. For example, in Australia and the United States you can easily buy do-it-yourself will-making kits. However, it is usually more reliable to get help from a professional, such as a solicitor or a public trustee, to ensure that your will is completed properly. If it is not completed properly, or does not comply with local state law, your will may be invalid when you die. You can find more advice on making a will in Australia here: https://moneysmart.gov.au/wills-and-powers-of-attorney. If you are in the UK, you can find more information here: www.gov.uk/make-will. If you are in the United States, the website advising you on will-making will depend on which state you reside in.

Here is an example:

a. If your affairs are not complicated, you can buy a template on the internet for making a will that is relevant for your own country or federal state. If your affairs are more complicated, you will have to seek a will writer or solicitor.

b. Make an estimate of what you are worth. Your 'estate' is everything you currently own. This includes things like a house or car and what is in your bank and savings accounts. You should take away any debts or mortgages. Make sure that you write your will assuming you died yesterday and review it when your circumstances change.

c. Decide on who you want to get what. You can make a gift to a loved one or a charity of a fixed sum or a specific item such as a house. You then leave the residuary of your estate to a named person(s) or charity. Alternatively, you can give a fixed percentage of your estate (e.g. 'I give 10% of my estate to Steven'). You should give the full name and address of the person or charity (and its registration number) and make sure all the percentages add up to 100 per cent. Any legacies will only be paid after any deductions or debts have been paid.

d. Put at least two people in charge ('executors') who will carry out the wishes of your will when you die. If you want this to be a friend or family member then discuss it with them and let people know where your will is kept.

e. Your will should be signed and dated and witnessed by at least two other people who do not benefit from your will. Again, remember to let people know where your will is kept. It is also worth considering showing your will to a solicitor, to ensure that it has been completed correctly.

A related task you could also consider is making a Power of Attorney (i.e. appointing someone to manage your financial and legal decisions in the event that you are not able to do so), or nominating a beneficiary for your life insurance or pension fund.

> If you made a will, how did it go? Write down any reflections below.
>
> ....
>
> ....
>
> ....
>
> ....

7. Write a story about your own death (and perhaps enact it)

This will be a story that is either for your own eyes or to share with family members. Write it in the first person present tense as if it is happening now from a field perspective (that is, through your own eyes rather than observing it yourself). Write a step-by-step account using as many different senses as possible (e.g. what you see, what you feel, what you hear, what you smell). Be sure to focus on your specific fears (e.g. suffocating) and that it finishes at your death (and not an afterlife). Once you have written this story, it is important to read over it. For instance, you might record yourself reading it aloud and play back the recording regularly.

It's even better to role-play your death and to re-enact it as far as possible. For example, Rachel has previously lain in a coffin at the Sydney Festival of Death and Dying. Lying in the coffin for several minutes gave her an opportunity to imagine more vividly what death might be like, and she found the coffin more peaceful and less claustrophobic than she expected. She also owns a body bag, which she carried around Australia to various workshops on the topic of death and encouraged many therapists to lie in. Many of those who volunteered to be zipped up in the body bag found it less confronting than they had imagined. It may also prompt you to focus on what you want to get from life now.

If you were to write a story of your own death, what details would be important to include to address your own unique fears? How might you go about reading it over repeatedly? Could you re-enact it?

....

....

....

....

....

....

If you did complete this task, what actually happened? What did you learn?

··

··

··

··

8. Swedish death cleaning

Another task to consider is döstädning, which translates to 'death cleaning' in Swedish. In 2017, Margareta Magnusson published *The Gentle Art of Swedish Death Cleaning: How to Free Yourself and Your Family from a Lifetime of Clutter*,[2] which first introduced the concept to many people outside Sweden. Death cleaning is the process of shedding unnecessary belongings, decluttering and organizing your home and affairs, to make your life as joyful as possible before it comes to a close. This might include sorting valuables or heirlooms from unwanted belongings, donating items to charity, downsizing, and preparing necessary paperwork that your relatives will need in the event of your death. As well as a valuable task to face up to your own death, death cleaning is also very practical. When a loved one dies, family members are often left with the momentous task of sorting through the person's belongings, on top of the grief they are already struggling with.

---

2   Magnusson, M. (2017). *The Gentle Art of Swedish Death Cleaning: How to Free Yourself and Your Family from a Lifetime of Clutter.* New York, NY: Scriber.

Having to decide which of the dead person's belongings to keep and which to discard can often bring additional stress and guilt to the bereaved, who may be unsure of which items you would have wanted them to treasure, and which you would have no problem with them discarding. Death cleaning is a helpful solution to this.

As you declutter your home, know that you are taking one less burden off the shoulders of your loved ones when the time of your death comes. Think about what you would like to leave to your family members or friends after you die (and ensure you put this in writing for your executors), and what you would prefer them to not have to deal with. Remember that death can come at any time, so don't put off this task based on the assumption that you will have decades to tick it off. None of us is immortal. All of us can benefit from donating or discarding belongings which are not adding value to our lives.

Take a moment to think about how you might begin the process of 'death cleaning'. Where in your home might you start, and how could you make the task easier? For example, could you enlist someone's help, play music while you clean, or contact a community group to see if you can donate your unwanted belongings?

....

....

....

....

If you did practise some 'death cleaning', how did it go? What happened, and did it change your perspective on death?

....

....

....

....

9. Throw a party with the theme of death

David celebrated his 50th birthday party with an anti-necrophobia (and anti-superstitions) party. Guests were invited to come dressed as they wish to die. There was someone who played a funeral director who kindly measured people up for a coffin and discussed their wishes. There was even a coffin in the garden to try out, and, to welcome guests, an actor playing the Devil. His brother came as a very impressive Grim Reaper with an antique scythe. There was a jazz band which improvised on the Funeral March. In accordance with Greek culture, 'Obols' (made from chocolates) were provided to be put under one's tongue to pay the ferryman, Charon, to take the dead across a mythical River Hades in the garden. This was combined with being anti-superstitious so there were 13 chairs around a dinner table. There was a ladder to walk under and a mirror to smash. All guests reported having a good time. We are sure you can think of many equally fun exercises to overcome a fear of death while having a good party! Please post them on social media and let us know (#deathparty on Twitter @drdavidveale and @rachelemenzies).

You could also have a smaller dinner party for embracing death. Some of the best inspirations are from art and literature or symbols of death. The table can be re-created as a vanitas, a still-life painting popular in the 17th century. Vanitas depicted the transience of life and certainty of death (e.g. using images such as rotting fruit, wilting flowers, broken dishes, extinguished candles, empty glasses, smoke, hourglasses and skulls). These show the decay and fleeting nature of life. Your table could also be decorated by flowers and plants that symbolize death such as lies; poppies; chrysanthemum, rosemary, or cypress trees.

Your menu might be inspired by dishes associated with death. Thus, it could include:

a. a dish that is eaten or otherwise prepared by the diner with a mini scythe

b. a dish that depicts other symbols associated with death or impermanence, such as vultures, ravens, candles, skulls, clocks, or the colour black

c. a dish that invokes old stone, moss, red poppies, cypress trees
d. a cooked ram head
e. fermented foods (we don't call them rotting) including everything from aged beef, miso, kimchi, cheese, sauerkraut and stink heads
f. a dish that involves poisonous plants – either made to look like them or using a related plant that is not poisonous (e.g. apple for arsenic, tomato related to deadly nightshade)
g. a dish that involves triangles –in still life the triangle symbolizes Christ's life, death and resurrection.

Take a few moments to imagine what your own death-themed party might look like. Who would you invite? What food or activities might you organize? What might you wear?

....

....

....

....

If you did hold a death-themed party, how did it go?

....

....

....

....

10. Go to a death cafe

Death cafes are not-for-profit community events that involve a group of people sitting around a table and talking about death in an open and non-judgemental way. The death cafe movement started to introduce a space where people could comfortably talk about death, without feeling that death must be a taboo topic. Death cafes are often held in local cafes, where a group of strangers can share their thoughts and attitudes to mortality while nibbling on cake or sipping tea. Rachel has attended her local death cafe many times and has found it to be a memorable and interesting experience. Thousands of death cafes have been held around the world, in more than 70 countries. To find your nearest death cafe, visit the official website at www.deathcafe.com.

If you did visit your local death cafe, how did it go? Was it as bad as you thought it would be?

....

....

....

....

....

11. Consider organ donation after your death

You may like to consider registering as an organ donor, so that your body can continue to benefit other people even after you have died. Organs from just one donor can save up to eight lives. We would encourage you to be informed and make positive decisions and select to donate some or all of your organs and tissue to improve the health of others.

Again, for our purposes it is the process of making a decision and discussing it with your relatives that's important in freeing yourself from death anxiety.

The process of becoming an organ donor will differ depending on where you live. For example, in the UK, the 'opt out' system means that all adults agree to become organ donors when they die, unless they have made it known that they do not wish to donate. If you have not recorded an organ donation decision, it will be considered that you agree to donate your organs when you die. You can learn more about the UK system here: www.organdonation.nhs.uk.

In the United States and Australia, there is an 'opt in' system, meaning that you need to officially register your interest in becoming an organ donor before you die. Despite the majority of people in these countries supporting organ donation, only a minority of people have actually registered as a donor. If you have not done so before you die, it will be impossible for your organs to go towards saving somebody's life. In many countries with an 'opt in' system, it takes just a few minutes to register as a donor. If you live in the United States you can do so here: www.organdonor.gov/register.html.

If you live in Australia, you can do so through MyGov, or at https://donatelife.gov.au/register-donor-today.

What are your thoughts on organ donation? If you would like to be an organ donor, write down when you will go about registering for this.

....

....

....

....

....

....

If you completed this task, how did it go? Write down any reflections below.

....

....

....

....

....

....

12. Write out your funeral wishes

You can add your funeral wishes to your will or make it a separate document. It may be a bit of fantasy since your wishes may be impractical, and your family may ignore them, but remember it is the *process* of discussing and writing down your wishes that is important. There are user-friendly websites designed to help you plan your funeral, which are listed in the Appendix.

You might start by doing some research on funeral services which are relevant to your wishes and values. For example, would you prefer to be buried or cremated? If cremated, then what would you like to be done with your ashes? Whether you want to sprinkle them in the River Ganges, have them made into a diamond or vinyl record, or shoot them to the stars, write down your preferences and wishes about your final party (and make sure you leave money to pay for it!). This exercise will again help you think about your own mortality, as well as taking practical steps towards finalizing your funerary preferences.

The problem with cremation is that it can be the equivalent of a 500-mile car journey. It uses gas and emits carbon dioxide and other toxic gases into the atmosphere. Traditional burial is the main alternative to cremation. However, burial can be more costly, due to the expense of the casket, as well as the purchase of the burial plot. What's more, when it comes to environmental costs, the materials used in the coffin and placed under the earth may take a bigger toll than cremation. If the burial is located far away from the funeral home, then this too could easily produce more carbon dioxide, with several cars needed for people to reach the destination. Land shortages may also mean that burial is no longer a feasible option given our ever-growing population.

'Green' burials are an eco-friendlier alternative to traditional burials and cremation. The most eco-friendly burial involves a biodegradable coffin (such as cardboard, rattan or bamboo) in a woodland or natural burial ground. Other solutions being developed are alkaline hydrolysis (or 'water cremation'), a process which breaks down the body's tissues and bones into a fine and very white 'ash'. This is recognized to be more eco-friendly than traditional cremation. Another alternative is to consider donating your body to science for medical students and research scientists. For more information on eco-friendly burial options, you can look at the Appendix of this book.

Again, discussing your wishes and writing them down is important. If you do this, then your relatives may do something that you are not happy with. For example, they might arrange a religious funeral in an expensive coffin when you are a devout atheist and want a biodegradable coffin, or vice versa!

Here are our own examples.

Rachel says, 'I am registered as an organ donor, and I would like my death to be as eco-friendly as possible. I'm still on the fence about whether I would like a natural burial, or whether I would like to be cremated, and my ashes used to nurture the family veggie garden. If I die before I make up my mind, I would be happy for my family to choose whichever of those two options they would prefer. I want my funeral to be non-religious, and somewhere outdoors in nature. I really want to have a celebratory atmosphere rather than a sombre one, with people wearing bright colours instead of black. I want George Harrison's "All Things Must Pass" played at the service. I would also like a poem by Mary Oliver to be read, either "When Death Comes" or "The Summer Day". At the wake, I want a big feast of delicious Italian food, and for people to share stories about my life and laugh together.'

David says, 'I would like a non-religious celebration. For my funeral, live music is important to me. I love the idea of a New Orleans Jazz band in a procession to the funeral. Of course, it's over the top but start with something sombre like the "Funeral March" with much histrionic wailing and gnashing of teeth before going into something celebratory. As a saxophone player, I like music without vocalists getting all the attention so my favourites for my funeral are John Coltrane on tenor sax mashing up "My Favourite Things" and King Curtis on soprano sax doing "Soul Serenade" (as on *Live at Fillmore West*). For songs with vocalists, then I'd like my band Bedlam's songs "Feeling Good" and "Hold on I'm Coming". I'd like to be cremated with Talking Heads playing "Road to Nowhere". I'd like my ashes to be shared between two places: a) my clinic so they can be kept in the cupboard and taken out for exposure tasks for people with death anxiety to play with. So much better to overcome your fears of death with the ashes of the author of the book you are reading! It gives a whole new meaning to interactive media; b) my family's allotment or garden.' Warning: cremation ashes are a great fertilizer but are harmful to plants in an undiluted form. This is due to the fact that cremated ashes are extremely alkaline and have very high levels of sodium. One solution is to mix the ashes with 'Living Memorial' soil, which you can buy over the internet (www.livingmemorial.co.uk; https://letyourlovegrow.com). Alternatively, consider alkaline hydrolysis cremation described earlier.

What would you like at your own funeral? Who could you discuss this with to make your wishes known?

....

....

....

....

....

....

If you have completed this task, how did it go? Write down any reflections below.

....

....

....

....

....

13. Write your obituary or eulogy for your own funeral

Writing your own obituary or funeral eulogy is another task we recommend for exposing yourself to the idea of your own death. When you write it, make sure that it reads *as if* you had died yesterday. Write it in the third person ('he/she'), chronologically and in detail. Write what you did in your life and what you valued. This is often a very valuable task, because it helps you reflect on your own life and what is important to you. The details we choose to include in our obituary or eulogy have much to say about what we value deep down. For example, do we include details about how much money we earned, or the luxury car we owned? Or do we instead focus on the relationships we had with others, and the kind of partner, daughter/son or parent we were? If you do this task, it would be worth considering what you wrote when you reach the later chapter 'Living Life to the Fullest', when you will be asked to consider your values.

In addition to writing your own obituary purely for your own exposure task or reflection, you might also consider sharing it with loved ones, or keeping it in the same places as other important documents, such as your will or advance care directive (which we will discuss below). If you do intend to share your obituary with others, one big advantage is that you can make sure your record is accurate. For example, doctors are encouraged to write their own obituary for the *British Medical Journal* and to keep it up to date like a curriculum vitae that they write for job applications. Writing this in advance is then an enormous help to your executor or relative who will have to tell your mourners about your life and what it stood for. Of course, it doesn't guarantee that the people who give your eulogy or write your obituary won't put a different slant on your life! Tell your executor where you have filed your details about your life and discuss it with a close relative or friend. It's on Rachel and David's to-do list!

What do you hope your obituary or eulogy might say about you? Why might this task be useful to complete?

....

....

....

....

....

....

....

If you completed this task, how did it go? Write down any re-flections below.

....

....

....

....

14. Write out your end-of-life wishes

Considering your end-of-life wishes is another valuable task for freeing yourself from your fear of death, as well as serving a very practical purpose. This is referred to as a 'living will', or 'advance care directive' or plan. These are not just important for people who are elderly. At any age, you could experience a medical crisis or accident which leaves you unable to make your own healthcare decisions or communicate your wishes. This is why it is so important to plan for your healthcare while you are reasonably healthy and mentally able to consider your preferences and values regarding your treatment. These decisions might involve whether you would want to receive CPR (cardiopulmonary resuscitation), whether you would want to be placed on a ventilator or not, and your stance on artificial nutrition (such as being fed through a tube) and hydration (such as through intravenous fluid). It also includes how you would want to spend your time while dying, such as whether you would prefer to die at home or in hospital, whether you would like music to be playing (and if so, what), and who you would like by your bedside (or who you would not want there). For example, what is more important to you: being physically comfortable and pain free, or being mentally present and aware of your surroundings? People's preferences and values can be so different that it is important to consider your own, write them down, and share them with people you trust.

In most countries, a lawyer is not required for you to record your end-of-life wishes. However, it might be helpful to talk to your doctor or physician, in order to help you understand the different treatment options and decisions that you might have to consider.

If you are in the UK, you can make an 'advance decision' or 'living will' here: https://compassionindying.org.uk/choose-a-way-to-make-an-advance-decision-living-will.

If you are in Australia, you can find more information on writing an advance care directive (and template forms to complete) here: www.health.gov.au/health-topics/palliative-care/planning-your-palliative-care/advance-care-directive.

If you are in the United States, you will need to complete the relevant form for your specific state. You can find more information on your state's laws and relevant forms by contacting Eldercare Locator (https://eldercare.acl.gov).

What do you think would be important to you at the end of your life? For example, if you had the choice, would you prefer to die at home or in hospital? Who would you want to be in charge of your end-of-life decisions, if you weren't able to communicate? Make a plan for when and how you would go about making your living will or advance care directive.

....

....

....

If you did make a living will or advance care directive, how did it go?

....

....

....

....

15. Paint or make your coffin

This might be part of a death-themed festival, workshop or club where members gather to build or paint their own coffins. Groups known as 'coffin clubs' have been created to help beginners create and decorate their own coffin or casket. These groups can currently be found in the UK, Australia and New Zealand. If you already have some knowledge of carpentry, you can buy or download casket blueprints online. Some websites, such as www.CasketPlans.com, also sell simple casket construction kits including all necessary materials; the wooden pieces simply slot into place, with no tools required.

Once your coffin is complete, you may choose to store it in your garage or a similar storage space, until your time comes. If you want to really embrace your mortality, you might like to keep the coffin within eyesight in your own home. Some people who build their own coffin end up using it as a coffee table in their living room, which certainly makes for an interesting conversation starter with guests. Rachel's father is currently having his own casket made (the apple clearly doesn't fall far from the tree). He plans to use the body of the casket as his desk in his clinic, while the lid is designed to be used as a bookshelf, with shelves that can be removed when the time comes. Of course, you may have more discreet plans for your own coffin (and if your artistic skills are not great, you may decide not to show off your hand-painted coffin in your living room). The goal with this task is to start to face your own mortality in whatever way is effective for you.

If you would like to paint your own coffin, how would you go about this? Are there coffin clubs near you, or could you enlist a handy friend to help you? Where might you keep the coffin afterwards?

....

....

....

....

If you did complete this task, how did it go? How did it feel to paint your own coffin, and did it change your perspective on death at all?

....

....

....

....

16. Anti-superstitious tasks

To strip intrusive thoughts and images of their assumed 'power', we recommend a positive pursuit of anti-superstition, to the point of *trying* to make bad things happen in your head, and in writing, to show that it can't be done. For example, if you're worried about the numbers 13 or 666, make a goal of asking for 13 in various transactions and have pictures of 666 in your bedroom. They're just numbers! They may now have an *association* with a past memory of a bad experience like death. Make those intrusive thoughts and images worse than they were in the first place. Kill off your loved ones in your mind. Imagine yourself being in a parallel world. Imagine your hands strangling your loved ones. Whatever you fear, just do it in your mind and make it worse. Show your internal bully who is in charge: you are not afraid of thoughts or pictures in your mind. Bad things do occasionally happen to all of us, but by chance, not because we have willed it or 'tempted fate'. We have demonstrated this approach for you by trying deliberately to make bad events happen to ourselves and our loved ones:

I wish that my wife, Elizabeth, my two daughters, Camilla and Rebecca, and I will die in a horrific car crash.
1 August 2021, David Veale

I wish that my husband Lachlan will die after being hit by a car while crossing the road. I wish that I will die a long, slow death after being diagnosed with a terminal illness.
1 August 2021, Rachel Menzies

Trauma work

Lastly, in addition to the exercises we have described here, it is also worth commenting on trauma work. Have you had any experiences or images of death in a close relative or friend that have been traumatic or bad? This would make your fears very understandable and likely to be still influencing the present. If there are aspects of their death you are avoiding, then you may benefit from seeing a therapist to talk through these issues or use imagery to re-experience them (called imagery rescripting or eye movement desensitization and reprocessing) and understand how the past is still influencing the present. This is very likely to contribute to some of the beliefs and feelings that you have now and may be maintaining your fear of death. You might want to talk to your family doctor or a therapist to see if this might be relevant.

Do you feel that trauma work would be relevant for you? If so, it might be worth considering seeing a therapist to address your trauma specifically.

....

....

....

....

Ali first decides to visit a cemetery, which he usually avoids. He pushes himself to look for graves of people who have died around the age he is now. He notices himself getting anxious whenever he spots someone who has died at his age, but finds that the anxiety settles down the longer he walks through the cemetery. Next, he decides to write his own obituary, as though he has just dropped dead the previous day from a heart attack. Lastly, Ali does some research online about his different burial options. Then, he sits down with his wife and talks about the kind of funeral he wants, and how and where he wants to be buried. Although this feels a little uncomfortable at first, and his wife is a little hesitant, he is happy that he is able to get through the conversation. Ali has slowly begun to accept his own death.

Sasha chooses exposure tasks that will help her overcome her fear of her loved ones dying. For example, she starts off by watching the television show *After Life*, which explores a man coping with his wife's death. She finds this confronting to watch at first, but finds that each episode becomes easier to watch. Sasha then decides to sit down with her parents and talk about what they want to happen to them when they die. However, when she tries to have this conversation, she discovers that her parents do not want to talk about it. She thinks about how to overcome this obstacle. In the end, she decides to practise exposure by imagining her parents dying instead, since they are not willing to talk about it with her. She starts off by writing a vivid and detailed story of her mother being diagnosed with cancer, being moved to palliative care at their local hospital, before eventually dying. She also includes her mother's imagined funeral in her story, including a description of herself delivering the eulogy. She records herself reading the story out loud and plays the recording back twice a day for a week. Although she is teary the first few times, over the week, she finds the story becomes less and less upsetting. She begins to come to terms with the realization that her parents will not be alive forever and starts to feel as if she might be able to cope when that day comes.

Julie chooses to create a will, which her husband has been encouraging her to do since her initial cancer diagnosis. She makes an appointment to see her solicitor. Although she does feel some anxiety discussing her will, she realizes that it is not as bad as she has expected it to be. In fact, she is surprised that she actually felt calmer about her own death after doing this, realizing that she now knows what will happen to all of her belongings and assets after she dies. After having this meeting, Julie also looks into death cleaning. She slowly starts getting rid of her possessions so that her children and husband aren't left to do this after her death. Again, Julie is surprised that this is easier than expected; she actually feels proud, knowing that she is doing something that will help her family cope with her death. She also starts having more conversations with staff in the palliative care team. Julie realizes that avoiding these tasks for so long has fed her anxiety and stopped her taking matters into her own hands.

Troubleshooting

Exposure tasks can at times be confronting and it is normal for challenges to arise as we are tackling these exercises. While most people usually notice a reduction in their anxiety over the first few exposure practices, some people may find that their anxiety is not budging. If you find that this is the case, the following questions may be useful to consider:

1. *Am I waiting long enough before stopping the exposure exercise?*
   Remember that you need to persist with the exposure to fully tolerate it. Make sure that you are only stopping the exposure task when you feel that you are better able to tolerate the anxiety.
2. *Have I stopped doing all of my safety-seeking behaviours and/or compulsions?*
   Remember that for exposure to work, it is important to stop doing any of your usual safety-seeking behaviours and

compulsions. This also includes subtle avoidance behaviours, such as distracting yourself, or being under the influence of a substance while you are carrying out the exposure exercise. If you are still doing these during the exposure, or even immediately afterwards, this may explain why your anxiety is not reducing between sessions.

3. *Have I stopped doing mental compulsions like prayer, counting, repeating certain phrases and mentally replaying situations?*
   Remember that mental rituals can sometimes be harder to notice, and can be a lot more subtle and automatic. For example, if you have noticed that you reassure yourself during the exposure task (e.g. by telling yourself, 'Everything is okay' or, 'I'll go to heaven when I die anyway'), we encourage you to do the opposite (e.g. instead telling yourself, 'Maybe there isn't actually a heaven').

Given that exposure can at times feel difficult and overwhelming, it is normal to occasionally lose motivation or doubt whether the hard work will be 'worth it'. If this is the case, first remember that the decision as to whether or not you do exposure therapy is completely up to you. Only you can choose which path to take when it comes to your anxiety: the path of continuing to avoid anything that brings you anxiety, or the path of facing up to these fears which have begun to overwhelm your life. It might be helpful to write out a list of pros and cons of each of these two paths, and to consider which is more likely to lead to happiness and contentment in the long term. Second, remember that exposure therapy has a lot of research to back it up – a number of studies show that it is the most effective way of overcoming death anxiety. It may feel difficult, but it is likely to help reduce your fears, if you can 'ride out' the anxiety which arises. Lastly, remember that death will happen whether or not you decide to face it and prepare for it. When you die, you will have a funeral, your body will be either buried or cremated, and your belongings will be dealt with by those you leave behind, regardless of whether you made any plans along these lines. Would you like to have a say in these decisions while you can, and increase the chances of having your values respected and your wishes carried out? Consider the advice attributed to the Stoic philosopher Musonius Rufus: 'Choose to die well while you can; wait too long, and it might become impossible to do so.' Seize this moment as a chance to practise accepting death, and doing what you can now to give yourself (or others) the kind of death you would be happy with.

Key points

- Facing your fears about death by doing death-related exercises or activities is an important start in overcoming your anxiety.
- Activities such as preparing a will, writing your own eulogy and discussing death with other people may not only help you overcome your fear, but also empower you to take control over your own death, rather than living in denial or avoidance.
- It is normal to feel anxious while completing these exercises; remember that the goal is to learn to tolerate this anxiety.

CHAPTER 8

Living Life to the Fullest

Living an enjoyable and meaningful life is not something that happens accidentally. Often, when you talk to people about what truly makes their life worth living, they will mention the small moments that they savour each day. Enjoying your morning coffee, going for a walk in the fresh air and feeling the sun on your face, sharing a joke with a friend, checking out the latest action film at the cinema, or enjoying a delicious meal at a local cafe – this is the stuff of life, and the list could go on and on!

So often, anxiety robs people of their opportunity to enjoy their lives, to expand their experiences and to truly make the most of their precious time on earth. Becoming caught up in your worries often distracts you from pursuing activities that give you a sense of enjoyment or satisfaction. Over time, your anxiety steals so many moments of your life that you can never get back.

Living life to the fullest involves making a commitment to pay more attention to your everyday experiences, to actively pursue enjoyable and meaningful opportunities each day, and to look for and appreciate the beauty and good fortune around you.

There are so many incredible moments we can have in our time on earth, if only we go after them!

Planning enjoyable activities

Although it may sound simple, decades of research show that including more enjoyable activities into our life is one of the most effective things we can do to improve our overall mood. Making time to do things which you have avoided or find enjoyable and satisfying will help improve how you feel day-to-day. And when your mood is better, you will be better equipped to deal with anxiety, negative thoughts and the general challenges of life that come up for everyone. This is particularly important for people who feel that they have stopped doing fun activities that they used to love or have started to neglect activities that used to give them a sense of achievement, however small (such as household chores, gardening, working or learning something new). Alternatively, you may be doing some things excessively as a way of trying to avoid difficult feelings. For example, you may be sleeping a lot during the day, spending all your time playing computer games or on social media for no particular reason. Others may spend their time ruminating and thinking excessively about death and not engaging in life. A crucial factor is building in routine to your pattern of sleeping and eating, and getting up at a regular time which is more or less in sync with the sun.

Take a moment to reflect on some activities that might give you a sense of enjoyment or achievement. If it is hard to think of some ideas, perhaps reflect on what you used to enjoy doing in the past, such as in your teenage years, or at times when you have felt happier than you do at the moment.

....

....

....

....

....

....

....

Planning activities

Part of feeling good is about planning and carrying out activities that we enjoy. If we don't consciously plan these, we can easily get caught up in errands and work, and find little time for our own happiness. Take a look at the following schedule for the next week. First, write down any things that are fixed into your schedule for the week, such as appointments or work. Next, try to fill in some of the free space with activities that you would enjoy. Try to include a balance of activities you would find enjoyable (such as watching a movie) as well as activities that would give you a sense of satisfaction or achievement (such as going to the gym, or doing a task you have been putting off).

If your schedule is already quite busy, consider including some avoided or enjoyable activities that might not take up much time. For example, on your lunch break, you might go for a short walk and listen to music. Or, you might spend five minutes before work sitting in the sunshine and sipping a cup of coffee. Even on your busy days, try and still make time to push yourself to do things purely for your own enjoyment, or to tackle tasks you have avoided.

	Morning	Afternoon	Evening
Monday			
Tuesday			
Wednesday			
Thursday			
Friday			
Saturday			
Sunday			

Now that you have drawn up this activity plan, try to stick to your plan as closely as possible. That being said, it is also important to be flexible. Sometimes things come up and our schedule doesn't go to plan, and this can make things challenging for anyone. What matters is that you keep working on doing enjoyable activities in whatever way is realistic for you.

Building a meaningful life

Decades of research tell us that finding purpose and meaning in life is important in improving our general mental health. If you are spending all day trying to sort out what happens when you die, it's important to focus on the life that you have left.

Identifying and living in line with our values is one way of doing this. Why might this be the case? First, considering our values can help us make more effective choices, particularly in terms of our unhelpful behaviours (e.g. substance use, avoidance, overspending, isolation, relationship conflict). Acting in accordance with our values can also help counter unpleasant feelings by making us feel empowered. When we live in line with our values, we are more likely to feel at peace with ourselves and our decisions, and to generally feel better about ourselves, than when we stray from our valued path. Research has shown that therapies which help people identify and behave in accordance with their values can help improve a number of different mental health conditions, such as depression, anxiety, chronic pain, PTSD and other conditions.

What's more, building a meaningful, values-based life can be particularly helpful for freeing yourself from the fear of death. For many people, the idea of death can make day-to-day life feel completely pointless. Lots of people who suffer from death anxiety describe feeling a deep sense of meaninglessness or lack of purpose. Others feel demotivated or lost. Many people find that their anxiety has become so overwhelming that it has stopped them from doing things that used to give them a sense of meaning, such as spending time with loved ones, pursuing their hobbies or talents or giving back to the community. This avoidance of activities further robs them of the chance to build a sense of purpose and further deepens their belief that their life is meaningless.

Many studies have shown that people who feel their life has purpose tend to worry less about death. By the same token, people who lack a feeling of meaning are much more likely to feel sad or worried at the thought of death. If we want to build a life that we find meaningful, the first step is to figure out what we care about the most.

What are values?

Values are about the kind of person we want to be in the world. How do we want to behave? How do we want to interact with others? How do we want to act at work, or spend our free time?

It is important to understand that values are not the same as goals. Goals are essentially tasks that can be 'ticked off' or achieved. Values are an ongoing process we might strive for, but cannot ever be 'achieved'. You might strive to be compassionate, but you can never 'tick off' compassion. Instead, you might be continually making moment-to-moment choices that are compassionate, such as calling a friend who is upset or volunteering for a cause. Goals are like the destinations we reach on our journey of life, whereas values are the compass directions themselves that guide that journey.

Values should be things that we choose freely and independently. Just because family members or friends hold certain values, that does not mean that we need to live in line with those values too. In fact, if we try to live our life by following other people's values, ignoring our own, we are likely to end up feeling frustrated, disappointed or unfulfilled. This is why it's important to try and identify what you yourself truly value. This can be a difficult task. If you have been raised in a family that places a strong emphasis on a value, how can you figure out whether you really share this value deep down, or whether you are only really wanting to follow your family's suit?

One thing that can be helpful in trying to identify your authentic values is to try and imagine what you would still care about and pursue if nobody were watching. For example, let's say you are trying to figure out whether you really value 'creativity'. At the moment, you might spend time in creative pursuits, such as playing in a band or painting. Now let's imagine that nobody knew about any of these activities. Your family, friends and co-workers have no idea about any of these creative endeavours. Would you still pursue this? Would you still spend your time painting and playing music if nobody would ever know? If the answer is yes, then creativity seems to be something you authentically value (if we would strive for a value regardless of whether others are watching, this suggests we are not doing it to seek other people's approval). If the answer is no, then it's unlikely that you really value creativity. And this is perfectly fine. There are hundreds of values we could choose from, and there are no 'right' or 'wrong' ones. One person might value excitement or wealth very highly, whereas these values might be of little importance to somebody else. You don't need to judge or justify your values; you are free to choose whichever values you like.

Identify your values

Here are some common values. Keep in mind that not all of them will be relevant to you and remember that there is no such thing as 'right' or 'wrong' values. All of us will have different values. For each value, select how important it is to you (*not very* important, *quite* important or *very* important). Try not to worry about what values you think you 'should' choose or picking something that just 'sounds good'. Instead, try to respond honestly based on what you think actually matters to you.

Values	Not very important	Quite important	Very important
Acceptance			
Adventure			
Ambition			
Assertiveness			
Authenticity			
Beauty			
Caring			
Challenge			
Commitment			
Compassion			
Conformity			
Connection			
Contribution			
Cooperation			
Courage			
Creativity			
Curiosity			
Dedication			
Discovery			
Enthusiasm			
Equality			
Excitement			

cont.

Values	Not very important	Quite important	Very important
Fairness			
Fitness			
Flexibility			
Freedom			
Friendliness			
Forgiveness			
Fun			
Generosity			
Gratitude			
Hard work			
Honesty			
Humility			
Humour			
Imagination			
Independence			
Intimacy			
Justice			
Kindness			
Knowledge			
Leadership			
Love			

Values	Not very important	Quite important	Very important
Mindfulness			
Open-mindedness			
Order			
Patience			
Persistence			
Playfulness			
Power			
Prosperity			
Respect			
Responsibility			
Romance			
Safety			
Self-awareness			
Self-care			
Self-development			
Sensuality			
Sexuality			
Skilfulness			
Spirituality			
Supportiveness			
Trust			

Working on your values

Choose three values from the above list that you consider to be very important to you. For this task, it might help to choose values where you feel you have room for improvement, rather than values which you feel you have been very successful with lately. Spend some time considering how in line your life currently is with these three values, what you would gain if you worked on living in line with these, and what steps you can take to make your life more congruent with these values. If possible, try and make these steps concrete and specific. For example, if your value is 'self-development', a step towards that value might be listening to a new podcast each week, downloading an app to learn a new language or scheduling time each evening to reflect on your day and how you could improve.

Value: ....

Is this value consistent with my life currently? Why/why not?

....

....

....

....

....

What would be different if I lived more in line with this value?

....

....

....

What steps can I take in the next month to be more in line with this value?

....

....

....

Value: ....

Is this value consistent with my life currently? Why/why not?

....

....

....

....

....

What would be different if I lived more in line with this value?

....

....

....

What steps can I take in the next month to be more in line with this value?

....

....

....

Value: ....

Is this value consistent with my life currently? Why/why not?

....

....

....

....

....

What would be different if I lived more in line with this value?

....

....

....

What steps can I take in the next month to be more in line with this value?

....

....

....

Over the next month, work on living in line with the three values you have chosen. Try and implement the actions or behaviours that you identified in this exercise, and see what impact this has. For example, do you notice any changes in your mood, your quality of life or your sense of purpose? What did you learn from this experience of living a values-based life?

Example: Julie reads over the list of values and identifies these three values as being particularly important to her: knowledge, connection and kindness. She realizes that although these things feel important, her cancer diagnosis, her fatigue and her anxiety have got in the way of her practising these values over the last few years. For example, Julie has been an avid reader, but her anxiety and her 'chemo brain' have made it harder to concentrate and enjoy books these days. Although connection is important to her, she has come to avoid being with other people during her anxious episodes. And while she considers herself a kind person, she has to admit that her avoidance has made it difficult to spend time with friends the way she would have liked.

So, Julie decides to work on these values. For 'knowledge', her goals are to listen to the news for five minutes each morning and to read one book each month. Julie knows that this second goal will be a challenge, so she thinks about how to make it more realistic for her. One idea she has is to join a local book club, which she knows will help her feel accountable. She also starts to listen to audiobooks while she goes for walks, which helps her goal be achievable. For 'connection', Julie decides to slowly start doing more activities with other people. For example, her first goal is to go out for lunch with her two children, to catch up with how they have been. After that, she plans a romantic night out at the movies with her husband, something they have not done in years. Finally, for 'kindness', Julie decides to call a friend of hers who has been going through a difficult time, and offer her support. She also chooses to give one compliment each day, particularly to her husband and children. After slowly ticking off her goals over the month, Julie begins to feel a sense of accomplishment. Although she has often felt that her life is empty and purposeless since her cancer returned, working on her values really does give her a sense of meaning. She has come to look forward to the time she schedules to sit down and expand her knowledge, the joy she feels from deep conversations with her loved ones, and the good feeling she gets when she says something kind to another person, even if they are a stranger. Life has started to feel worth living.

Values: a life's work

Remember that, unlike goals, values cannot be 'ticked off'. Striving towards our values is a lifelong process of ongoing action, but one that is likely to increase our sense of meaning and fulfilment in life. So, it is important to make a commitment to continue working on living in line with your own values.

Maintaining and building relationships

Before we talk about the importance of relationships, we need to understand a little bit about our species. Humans are inherently social creatures. For thousands of years, close relationships have been essential for our survival. Early homo sapiens lived in tight-knit social groups. We hunted and gathered food together, and we relied on our fellow humans to protect us from predators and other threats. The odds of an early human surviving on their own, without the assistance and protection of a group, were extremely slim. As a result, humans who were unable or unwilling to maintain close relationships died off quite quickly. Instead, those who were highly motivated to build social ties lived long enough to reproduce, and passed on their social traits to their offspring. So, across thousands of years of evolution, humans became wired with a strong need for social connections.

Today, we are not as different from our early ancestors as we might like to think. Although we may no longer rely as much on other people to protect us from *physical* threats, such as tigers or bears, we do rely on them for a whole host of other things. In particular, our relationships with our nearest and dearest play a key role in how we deal with *emotional* threats, such as feelings of sadness, anxiety and anger.

So how important are our relationships to how we feel? Researchers at Harvard University have conducted one of the longest-running studies into human happiness. Since 1938, the study has followed the lives of more than a thousand people. Each year the researchers have interviewed these men and women, looked through their medical records and blood tests, even interviewing their spouses and children. They were determined to find out the secret to a happy life. After more than 80 years, what have they found? Is happiness in your genes, your income or your IQ? Is the key to contentment in the amount of exercise you do, or in a successful career? Their results are fascinating: by far the biggest predictor of a long and happy life is the quality of your relationships. Having strong, supportive relationships with other people protects you not only from mental health problems, it even seems to impact your physical health. By knowing how happy a person was in their relationships when they were 50 years old, researchers could even predict how physically healthy that person would be at age 80.

So, being connected with yourself and others is central to keeping yourself happy and healthy. What's more, relationships are also crucial to keeping the fear of death at bay. Several studies have shown that people who feel secure in their relationships are less troubled by the thought of death. So much so, that researchers see our attachments to other people as one major *buffer* against death. This means that although our connections with others are important for all of us, they may be even more important for people who experience a strong fear of death. And, it is the quality of our relationships, not the quantity, that seems to be important. Having strong, caring friendships with a handful of trusted people seems to be more vital than having a large social circle of people by whom you do not feel very supported.

Taking care of relationships is a bit like caring for a garden. Any plant that doesn't get at least some care, in the form of a small sip of water every so often, will eventually die. If you don't put time or effort into tending plants, regularly fertilizing, watering and pruning them, there is a small chance that a hardy plant will tolerate it and survive. But even if it survives neglect, it won't thrive, and it certainly won't be as healthy or long-lasting as a plant which you devote a lot of attention and care to. Relationships are very similar. It is impossible for relationships to thrive if we don't put in time to cultivate them.

Fulfilling relationships rarely just *happen* to us. We don't usually stumble on close, supportive relationships by accident. Even if we first met someone through coincidental circumstances, this doesn't usually develop into a meaningful and supportive relationship by chance. Strong relationships take time and effort to grow. They almost always involve a process of making time to connect with one another, and investing effort in getting to know and support one another. This is why this section talks about *building* and *maintaining* relationships, rather than, say, just '*being* in relationships', which would sound quite passive. Making and keeping solid friendships is an active and deliberate process. There are two main steps involved in working on your relationships:

1. Attend to your existing relationships.
2. Increase your social involvement.

Attending to your existing relationships involves making a deliberate choice to reach out to current friends and family. This may include things like calling up or messaging an old friend, arranging to go out to lunch with a family member, or scheduling a date night with your partner. It may involve putting some time aside each week to prioritize your most important relationships. This is particularly the case if you know that you tend to withdraw from social plans when you are feeling stressed or when your mood is low.

Remember that the quality of the relationship really matters. For example, simply being in a romantic relationship with someone is not by default going to help a person's wellbeing (in fact, the Harvard study found that being single was often more helpful to overall health than being in an unhappy or unsupportive marriage).

If you are in a relationship which is not feeling fulfilling or has lost its spark, then striving to build connection, trust and satisfaction may be crucial here. Reaching out for professional support, such as a relationship counsellor or self-help guides which are tailored to relationships, may also be worth considering.

Sometimes, you may not have many (or any) existing relationships to attend to, which makes step one difficult. This is where the second step – increasing your social involvement – is essential. If you feel that your current social circle is smaller than you might like, it is vital to start becoming more involved in the community, to increase your opportunities to make new connections. This might include looking for groups in your area for people who share your hobbies, such as a local book club, bushwalking group or religious group. Websites such as Meetup.com are designed specifically to help you find groups of people near you with like-minded interests. Other things that get you involved in your community, such as joining a local support group or volunteering, are also worth considering. Every time you put yourself out there and get involved with new people, you increase your chances of finding like-minded people. With time and work, you might start to build a meaningful and supportive friendship that would never have existed had you not looked beyond your current social circle.

People in my circles

This exercise aims to help you identify people who are currently a part of your life, or who have been in the past. This is a useful first step when it comes to considering which relationships might be worth attending to, and who you might want to reach out to.

First, in the innermost circle (closest to 'me'), jot down the names of people who are currently important to you. These may be people you already are well connected to, and with whom you already have a strong relationship or see often.

In the second circle, write down the names of people who are currently in your life, but you aren't as close to as those in the first circle. For example, these may be people with whom you have a good relationship, but don't see quite as often.

Lastly, in the third and outermost circle, write down the names of people who have been supportive in the past, but with whom you no longer have contact. For instance, this could include people with whom you were once close, or were once supportive, but have lost touch with.

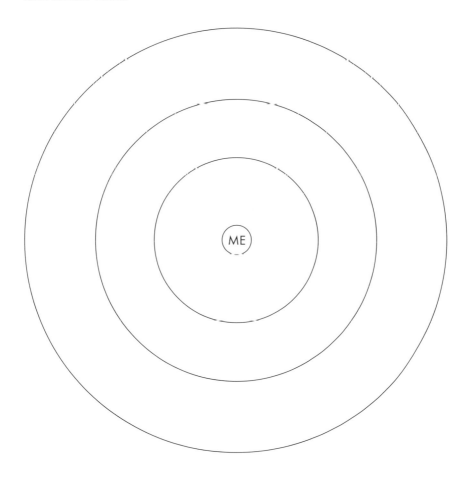

Attending to existing relationships

Now that you have written down some names, pick three relationships that you would like to work on cultivating. It is up to you which people you start with here. Perhaps you would like to pick three people in the outer circle, to try and reconnect with and rebuild past friendships that you once had. Alternatively, you might feel it is easier to start with people in your inner circles and work on improving the relationships that you are already in. You might even like to pick one name from each of the three circles.

Person 1:

....

....

....

Person 2:

....

....

....

Person 3:

....

....

....

Next, try and write down some concrete steps you could take in the next week or month to work on this relationship. This might include things like planning an activity with them, sending them a message to check in with how they're going, or doing something nice for them, such as paying them a compliment or offering to help support them with something they're going through. If this is an old former friend (such as someone from your third, outermost circle), it might be something as simple as contacting them to let them know that you have missed their company and would like to reconnect.

What specific steps could you take to cultivate this relationship?

Person 1:

....

....

....

Person 2:

....

....

....

Person 3:

....

....

....

Lastly, are there any obstacles that might get in the way? This might include things like living far away from the person, time restraints (both yours and theirs), unresolved conflict, or even feelings of anxiety about reconnecting with someone. Anticipating and brainstorming solutions to potential problems can be useful here.

Are there any barriers that might get in the way of you working on this relationship? If so, how might you address these obstacles?

Person 1:

....

....

....

Person 2:

....

....

....

Person 3:

....

....

....

Increase your social involvement

Earlier in this chapter, you reflected on activities which would give you a sense of enjoyment or achievement. In this exercise, the aim is to find activities which will give you an opportunity to meet new, like-minded people. For example, if you love volunteering, volunteering in a group setting (e.g. joining a group which meets weekly to assemble care packs for the homeless) is far more likely to lead to relationships than volunteering in a more individual way (e.g. assembling similar care packs on your own from your own home). While both are commendable and likely to be rewarding, your goal for this task is to help you build relationships (particularly if you feel that you do not have many existing ones at present).

Have a look through some of the suggestions for social activities below, and tick off the ones that interest you. We tend to get along well with people who share our interests, so prioritize choosing activities that most appeal to you (you might not make many friends at a book club if you hate reading). Ideally, try and look out for opportunities where the same group of people meet regularly, such as an ongoing language class, rather than a one-off social event. We are far more likely to build connections with people we see more often.

- ☐ A yoga or fitness class
- ☐ A board game club
- ☐ A volunteering group (e.g. a beach or street clean-up, tree-planting, or animal rescue group)
- ☐ A community garden
- ☐ A book club
- ☐ A language class or language conversation group
- ☐ A bushwalking club
- ☐ A sports team
- ☐ A religious group

- ☐ A writers' club
- ☐ A dance class
- ☐ A theatre or improv group
- ☐ An LGBT+ (lesbian, gay, bisexual, transgender and others) club
- ☐ A singles meetup
- ☐ A support group, such as an anxiety management group
- ☐ A philosophy discussion group
- ☐ A photography or painting class
- ☐ Other: ....
- ☐ Other: ....

Now that you have considered some social activities that might interest you, what are some concrete steps you can take in the next month towards increasing your social involvement? For example, this might include buying a membership to your local group fitness centre, or visiting your local community centre to see what relevant events are on offer. You might also like to consider exploring your neighbourhood's local social media page. For example, many suburbs have a Facebook page for residents, where people may enquire about local social events or clubs.

....

....

....

....

....

Are there any obstacles that might get in the way of you increasing your social involvement? For example, time or financial obstacles, or feeling anxious in a group environment? How might you manage or solve this problem? (For example, could you invite a friend or acquaintance to join you the first time you go?)

....

....

....

....

....

Rippling

Dr Irvin Yalom is a world-renowned therapist, who described the concept of 'rippling' as follows:

> Rippling refers to the fact that each of us creates – often without our conscious intent or knowledge – concentric circles of influence that may affect others for years, even for generations. That is, the effect we have on other people is in turn passed on to others, much as the ripples in a pond go on and on until they're no longer visible but continuing at a nano level... The idea that we can leave something of ourselves, even beyond our knowing, offers a potent answer to those who claim that meaninglessness inevitably flows from one's finiteness and transiency.[1]

1   Yalom, I. (2008). *Staring at the Sun.* Carlton North, Victoria: Scribe Publications, p.83.

Yalom worked extensively with terminally ill individuals for decades. He coined the term 'rippling' to describe the belief that 'one may persist, not in one's individual personhood, but through values and actions that ripple on and on through generations to come'. Yalom says:

> I think we ripple on into others, just like a stone puts its ripples into a brook. That, for me, too, is a source of comfort. It kind of, in a sense, negates the sense of total oblivion. Some piece of ourselves, not necessarily our consciousness, but some piece of ourselves gets passed on and on and on.[2]

The concept of rippling suggests that we can live on long after our death by leaving behind some part of ourselves, such as a trait or behaviour, a piece of wisdom or indeed a value. These may be passed on to others, for generation after generation, without us even being aware of it. Yalom describes himself as a living example of his own father's 'rippling', as he continues his father's tradition of always picking up the bill when he dines out with his family. When his children thank him, he reminds them, 'Thank your grandfather Ben Yalom. I'm only a vessel passing on his generosity.'

In one way or another, we are all carriers of the lessons and values we have taken in from others and made a part of ourselves. In light of that, what lessons and values will we pass on to others?

If you had to sit down and write a list, how many people would you have to thank for shaping you, bit by bit, into the person you are today? A childhood friend, for teaching you the meaning of loyalty; your Year 5 teacher, who encouraged you to always ask for help; a neighbour, who always went out of their way to greet you and taught you the importance of these small acts of kindness? There would likely be too many people to name, and, most

---

2   Interview with Irvin Yalom and David Van Nuys on the Wise Counsel podcast, published on 19 February 2008. Audio recording available here: https://podtail.com/en/podcast/wise-counsel-podcasts/irvin-yalom-on-death-anxiety

importantly, many of them would never even know the impact that they had on you. By the same token, how many people's lives have been shaped, even in some small way, by some action or gesture that you made?

This powerful idea of 'rippling' can help motivate us to truly live life to the fullest. We all have a wonderful opportunity to leave our mark on others, and by doing so, to live on after we are physically gone. By passing on acts of care and love, by doing good deeds and by imparting our knowledge, wisdom and values, to others, we can continue to exist in the world long after our death.

Take a moment to reflect on examples of 'rippling' in your own life. Who are some people who have helped shaped you, in one way or another, into the person you are today? This could range from seemingly small examples (such as a certain phrase you often say, that you learned from someone else) to bigger impacts (such as values you hold dear, which someone else inspired you to believe in).

Write down their names below, as well as how they have contributed to who you have become.

....

....

....

....

....

....

Now that you have considered how others' lives may have 'rippled' into your own, consider the opposite. Of course, we can never really know the infinite ways our thoughts and actions have shaped other people. But take a moment to imagine some examples of this. For example, have you helped a friend make a tough decision, inspired someone else to share or consider your own values, or even brought a moment of happiness to someone around you? How might these actions 'ripple on' to the lives of other people? Remember, if it is difficult to think of examples, that doesn't mean they aren't there. There are likely hundreds of ways in which each of us have touched the lives of others, and we may never be aware of most of these.

Can you think of some examples of how you may have touched others' lives, even in seemingly small ways? Write them down below.

....

....

....

....

....

....

....

....

Peter. In this exercise, Peter is able to think of lots of examples of other people's effects on him. He reflects on how his grandfather's love for cricket led to his own love for the sport, and a Year 10 English teacher whose lessons inspired him to become a writer. Peter also recalls lots of memories of his mother showing patience, such as the hours she spent tending plants in the garden, or when she often reminded him that 'slow and steady wins the race'. He suspects that her patience has rubbed off on him. Peter also considers himself to be someone who cares a lot about world issues; he is always reading the latest news, and values being well informed. When he thinks about where this comes from, he recalls a friend he met at university, who was very politically active, and often invited him to protests. Although he hasn't seen the friend in years, it occurs to him that he has her (and others) to thank for his interests today.

At first, Peter finds it hard to think about how he might have rippled on to others, especially because he found himself withdrawing from other people when his mood got worse a few years ago. He decides to start by considering his family. He knows that when he was a teenager, his younger sister looked up to him for his academic achievements at school, and he figures that he probably encouraged her to be diligent and work hard. Then he thinks about his friends. He tries to imagine what his friends might say if someone asks them how he has impacted them. He imagines that they might say he is always there when they need support, and often lends a non-judgemental ear. Perhaps this has rubbed off on them, and they are, in turn, more open and supportive when their other friends are in need? Peter also imagines that his friends would say he often passionately speaks to them about politics, and the importance of speaking out about causes you value. He figures that, just as his old friend influenced his own beliefs, his own views and attitudes have probably left a mark on his current friends. And surely, with his thousands of Tweets and social media posts, at least one has influenced the views of a stranger...

Peter realizes that even when he has physically died, traces of him will live on from generation to generation. His beliefs, his values and even some of his mannerisms will continue to affect the world in ways he can never predict. Although he does not have any children himself, it occurs to him that many of his friends do, and that just as he has left traces of himself on his friends, they might pass these on to their children. Peter also realizes that if he wants to keep 'rippling', he needs to actively interact with other people, rather than spending quite as much time isolating himself as he has been doing lately. He resolves to spend more time engaging with the world and people around him, so as to leave behind as many 'concentric circles of influence' (in Yalom's words) as he can.

Some final comments on living life to the fullest...

Building an enjoyable and fulfilling life can be, so to speak, a life's work. The strategies outlined in this chapter are the first step on this journey. By deliberately carving out time for enjoyable activities, working on your relationships, living in line with your values, and reminding yourself of the concept of 'rippling', you are well on track to building a fulfilling life. Each of these represent another tool in your toolbox to help you overcome your fear of death.

As you approach the end of this book, consider a thought experiment developed by the existential philosopher Friedrich Nietzsche. His novel, *Thus Spoke Zarathustra*, poses a challenge. He asks us to imagine that we have been told that we must live our own identical life over and over again for all eternity. Imagine, he says, that you must repeat every single moment of your life over and over, on an endless loop.

How would you feel on discovering this? Would you feel overjoyed to learn that you can experience for ever and ever the incredible, fulfilling life that you have lived? Or would you be disappointed or filled with despair to have to relive your life for all eternity?

As you consider this, be wary of feelings of regret, or of ruminating over your past. Remember that the past is over, and it is not something now within your control. Because of this, there is not much use stewing over mistakes made, or time wasted. Instead, turn your gaze to the future. What can you do now so that you may live the best version of your life? What steps can you take in the next month to start to build a life that you would be happy to repeat for eternity?

You have only one life. Live it fully and live it well.

Appendix

Survey of death-related beliefs and behaviours

If you would like to monitor your progress, it may be helpful to complete the following survey at the beginning of this book, and once again when you have made your way to the end. The survey focuses on unhelpful beliefs, and avoidance behaviours, related to death.

Below we have compiled a list of death-related thoughts, beliefs and attitudes that you may experience. We want you to indicate, by circling the number, how frequently you are troubled by each thought on a scale from 1 ('never have the thought') to 5 ('always have the thought').

	Never have the thought	Rarely have the thought	Sometimes have the thought	Often have the thought	Always have the thought
1. It would be terrible to not have time to experience everything I want to	1	2	3	4	5
2. It would be horrible to die alone	1	2	3	4	5
3. Death is no doubt a horrible experience	1	2	3	4	5
4. I couldn't cope with growing old without my loved ones	1	2	3	4	5
5. It would be awful if I died of a terminal illness	1	2	3	4	5
6. Life is far too short	1	2	3	4	5
6. My death will be a painful experience	1	2	3	4	5
7. I couldn't cope with growing old without my loved ones	1	2	3	4	5
8. It will be terrible to never think or experience anything again	1	2	3	4	5
9. I will lose a loved one suddenly and it will destroy me	1	2	3	4	5
10. On my deathbed, I will not be able to face death as bravely as I should	1	2	3	4	5
11. I wouldn't cope if someone I care for developed a fatal illness	1	2	3	4	5
Total					

Below we have compiled a list of activities that some people may avoid. Please indicate how frequently you would avoid each of these situations, on a scale from 1 ('I would never avoid') to 5 ('I would always avoid').

	Never avoid	Rarely avoid	Sometimes avoid	Often avoid	Always avoid
1. Watching or reading media stories about dying	1	2	3	4	5
2. Thinking about being diagnosed with a terminal illness	1	2	3	4	5
3. Reading a novel with a character who is dying	1	2	3	4	5
4. Thinking about a loved one dying	1	2	3	4	5
5. Watching a film or TV show with a character who is dying	1	2	3	4	5
6. Thinking about myself dying	1	2	3	4	5
7. Reading a memoir or essay by someone diagnosed with a terminal illness	1	2	3	4	5
Total					

Recommended books about death and dying

- Seneca (2005). *On the Shortness of Life*. London: Penguin. A translation of Stoic writings on accepting death by ancient Roman philosopher Seneca.
- Yalom, I.D. (2008). *Staring at the Sun: Overcoming the Terror of Death*. San Francisco, CA: Jossey-Bass. A guide for overcoming fears of death by existential psychotherapist Irvin Yalom.
- Doughty, C. (2017). *From Here to Eternity: Traveling the World to Find the Good Death*. New York, NY: Hachette. An entertaining and informative exploration of cultural attitudes to death across the world.
- Solomon, S., Greenberg, J. and Pyszczynski, T. (2015). *The Worm at the Core: On the Role of Death in Life*. London: Penguin. An exploration by three experts in social psychology on how death anxiety is the hidden motive behind most human behaviours.
- Doughty, C. (2015). *Smoke Gets in Your Eyes: And Other Lessons from the Crematorium*. Edinburgh: Canongate Books. A compelling account of the funeral industry and how our society can develop more healthy attitudes to death.
- Tanaka, K. (2014). *Everybody Dies: A Children's Book for Grown-Ups*. New York, NY: Harper Design. A humorous book which seeks to normalize death through illustrations and quirky games and activities.
- Doughty, C. (2019). *Will My Cat Eat My Eyeballs? And Other Questions about Dead Bodies*. London: Orion. A book for young people which answers questions about death submitted by children.
- Menzies, R.E., and Menzies, R.G. (2021). *Mortals: How the Fear of Death Shaped Human Society*. Sydney: Allen & Unwin. An exploration of how an unconscious fear of death is the hidden driver of most of humankind's endeavours.

Recommended websites about death and dying

- To create your own end-of-life or funeral plan – www.joincake.com
- The Order of the Good Death, an organization designed to normalize death, educate the public and increase society's acceptance of death – www.orderofthegooddeath.com
- YouTube channel 'Ask a Mortician', a collection of videos normalizing and explaining issues related to death – www.youtube.com/user/OrderoftheGoodDeath
- A series of photos showing people before and immediately after death, photographed by Walter Schels – www.walterschels.com/en/portfolios/portraits/album/8. An article describing this project, and giving brief descriptions of each of the individuals photographed by Schels, can be found here: www.theguardian.com/society/gallery/2008/mar/31/lifebeforedeath

Information on eco-friendly mortuary options

- 'A greener way to go: What's the most eco-friendly way to dispose of a body?' Article by Ammar Kalia, *The Guardian*, 10 July 2019. www.theguardian.com/lifeandstyle/2019/jul/09/greener-way-to-go-eco-friendly-way-dispose-of-body-burial-cremation
- Information on green burial in the United States – www.greenburialcouncil.org
- Information on green burials in the UK – www.naturaldeath.org.uk
- Information on green burials in Australia – www.gatheredhere.com.au/green-funerals-australia

Games and activities

- *The Death Deck* – A card game and conversation starter: www. thedeathdeck.com
- *Mortalls* – A card game and conversation starter: www.mortalls. com
- *Stupid Deaths: The Frightfully Funny Game* – A board game which seeks to normalize and lighten death by celebrating the most bizarre deaths in history.
- *A Mortician's Tale* – A mobile phone app in which you play as a funeral home worker, preparing bodies and attending funerals. Available on the Apple App Store.
- For information on how to host your own Death Over Dinner event – https://deathoverdinner.org
- For information on death cafes, and where to find your nearest event – www.deathcafe.com

Podcasts

- *The Dying Matters Podcast*. Listen on Apple Podcasts, Google Podcasts or Spotify.
- *Death in the Afternoon*. Listen on Apple Podcasts, Google Podcasts or Spotify.

About the Authors

Rachel Menzies completed her honours degree, master's and doctorate in psychology at the University of Sydney. She won the Dick Thompson Thesis Prize for her work on the dread of death and its relationship to obsessive compulsive disorder (OCD). Rachel was featured in *The Conversation Yearbook 2016*, a collection of the top 1 per cent of 'standout articles from Australia's top thinkers'. Rachel currently works as a clinical psychologist and a postdoctoral research fellow at the University of Sydney. She has published extensively on the fear of death and its role in mental health. This is her fourth book on the topic. Her website is www.rachelmenzies.com.

David Veale is a consultant psychiatrist in cognitive behavioural psychotherapies and leads a national outpatient and residential unit service for people with severe anxiety disorders at the South London and Maudsley NHS Trust. He is a visiting professor at the Institute of Psychiatry, Psychology and Neuroscience, King's College London. He was a member of the group that wrote the NICE guidelines on OCD in 2006 and chaired the NICE Evidence Update on OCD in 2013. He is an Honorary Fellow of the British

Association of Behavioural and Cognitive Psychotherapies, a Fellow of the British Psychological Society and a Fellow of the Royal College of Psychiatrists. He is a trustee of the UK charities OCD Action, the Body Dysmorphic Disorder Foundation and Emetophobia Action. His website is www.veale.co.uk.

Index